BEYOND TILL DEATH DO US PART

SURVIVING SPOUSAL LOSS AND EMBRACING NEW BEGINNINGS

CINDY BARBER-ROBERTS

TABLE OF CONTENTS

FOREWORD

All names and places have been changed. The stories are
fictitious and just used as examples.

Acknowledgment

I want to thank my husband for being patient when I decided I had to write no matter what time of day it was, and for understanding the need to write about the loss of my first husband. Your love and support enabled me to get through this loss and still be able to function. And to my children, who were there when it happened. God knows I would not have been able to make it without you all. Thank you for being there, and thank you to everyone who stayed there.

And to all the firefighters and the families that support you, it is with great will that we watch you walk out that door for a call and hold firm until you return. God bless you for all you do for your communities and families. This book is dedicated to each and every one of you.

1

THE REALITY OF SUDDEN LOSS

"The hardest goodbyes are the ones we don't get to say."

We were watching TV, and the call came over the radio. You jumped into action and headed out the door, but just before you left, you said, "You know I love you and always will." And I looked back at you and said, "I love you too." Those were the last words we ever spoke to each other. I'm so glad they were words of love and kindness because everything would change in the next hour of my life.

I thought it odd that my husband told me he loved me before he left. Don't get me wrong, we said it to each other all the time, but not usually when he was heading out the door for a fire call.

The night had started with each of us getting home from work, and we were happy and excited because the topic of conversation that night was a cruise, which we had coming up in just a couple of months. We were in the kitchen cooking dinner together, and you grabbed me and swung me around and said, "We must learn how to salsa dance. We want to show the kids that we have been practicing." We danced for a few minutes, and since dinner was ready, we sat down. After dinner, you said you were going to take a bath and lie down. But you decided to join me when you got out of the tub, and I was still sitting there and watching TV. We did this for about 30 minutes before the call came in. And the rest, they say, is history.

I heard a knock at my door. My friend was there and said, "I need you to come with me to the hospital. They have taken Dene to the hospital with what we think may be heat exhaustion." I was frightened by this immediately. I grabbed my things, and off to the hospital we went. While we were going, I heard her radio go off and say, we need another responder for the box. I wasn't sure if they were talking about the ambulance or what was happening. My friend quickly turned her radio down. As we approached the hospital, the Chief's and Assistant Chief's trucks passed before us, with an ambulance leading the way. My heart sank. I knew that was my husband in there, and it must be serious for them both to be going to the hospital at the same time.

Once we got to the hospital, I walked into the emergency room and heard them call a code blue. I immediately knew that it was for my husband. I ran to the desk and told the lady there they were bringing my husband in, and I needed to go back there. She took a moment and told me to come with her to a room, and as we were going to the room, I saw them bring my husband in, and the Dr. was on his chest doing CPR. I knew things were bad. I started praying as quickly as I could to please let him be okay. I started sobbing, and I just needed to see him! They wouldn't let me because they were working on him, which is what they told me. After about 25 minutes or so, my husband's best friend came to me and told me he didn't make it. He had coded in the ambulance and was DOA when they arrived at the hospital but had to try when the Dr was there. It didn't work. My world just fell entirely apart right then, right there. I didn't know what to do. I didn't know what to say or who to call. My thoughts were so chaotic that I couldn't understand anything at that moment. My son was there and told me to call his sister, who was on the road headed to her college graduation, which was supposed to be the next day. She had someone driving with her, so I called and told her what happened, and she headed back right then. All our worlds changed at that moment. Where do we go from here?

My entire life changed that night. I didn't want to go back home. I didn't want to go to a hotel. I wanted to stay in the hospital. There in that room with him. I wasn't ready to let go. I didn't believe he wouldn't wake up and smile and say, "Just kidding!" He was quite a jokester. No, this couldn't be real. This was all a bad dream, and I would wake up soon.

But I never woke up. It wasn't a dream. It was real, and now, I had to figure out how to navigate this life without the person I thought I would grow old with.

So, as you can see, your responses change so quickly when it is a sudden death. It's hard to figure out what you are feeling at that moment. I do know that I didn't want to believe them. I wanted it not to be true. I wanted them to tell me he was going to be okay. I realized it wouldn't change soon after I felt this way. This was happening, and I had to figure it out from here. My disbelief cracked, and the hurt rushed in. The anger rushed in. The guilt rushed in. So many emotions in such a short time.

You begin thinking about that last interaction between you both. Did he know something was wrong, and that's why he told me he loved me right before he left? Did he not tell me he was hurting or not feeling well for some other reason? The conversation at dinner that night, the conversation about the cruise. I certainly don't feel like he knew what was coming. We had such a beautiful evening. Was this God's way of giving me a last memory? Again, questions, questions, questions. Questions that would never be answered. But you learn to quit asking those questions and deal with the emotions as they come.

Every loss is a tragic loss. And there isn't a certain kind of grief that you may or may not feel. You didn't get to see them slowly slip away. You didn't get to have those last conversations. You didn't have time to apologize for the little things you knew drove them crazy. It's a free fall of emotions. Hang on for the ride because it's going to be a rough one.

Your grief isn't just about the person you lost; it's about all the things that won't happen now. The milestone anniversaries, the trips that you had planned. The golden age that you were looking forward to enjoying together. They won't see their grandchildren grow up. They won't see how great the adult children end up doing in their lives. The memories you have are the only ones you will have. There won't be new ones to make. It's a tough pill to swallow when all this is realized.

A case study done in the late eighties examined whether older adults' psychological adjustments to widowhood would vary based on a spouse's suddenness or anticipated death. They sampled two hundred and ten widows who participated in a study called "Changing Lives of Older Couples (CLOC).

These participants were sixty-five and older and were interviewed at six months, eighteen months, and 48 months after spousal death. Overall, the study showed that many of the persons interviewed were not as affected by sudden death with no warning. Those who suffered prolonged illnesses seemed to suffer from an elevated anxiety level at the six-month and eighteen-month intervals. It was also found that sudden death was associated with higher yearning levels in women but much lower in men.

So those findings bring us to question the favored belief that grief is more severe if it is sudden but suggests a more complex relationship between circumstances of spousal loss.

We know that grief manifests itself in many ways. Physical ways can vary from fatigue to premature death. Powerful emotions such as helplessness, hopelessness, anxiety, sadness, and anger can show up. Learning how to handle these emotions as they arrive is something we should be aware of. Our friends and family should also be mindful of these emotions and be there to help us to navigate these feelings. Fatigue and withdrawal are signs of depression and anxiety. Be cognizant of these feelings, and don't fall into the abyss before adapting to changing your behavior or seeking help. The bed may feel like it's just too big or too empty. This could cause you to be sleepless. You may lose the ability to eat like you should just because you don't feel like eating. Things that may have meant a lot to you in the past may not seem so important now. These are the kinds of things that family and friends should help us to watch out for. Sometimes, they can see it better than we can.

Immediate support is needed. When you are in the shadows of pain, the light of support becomes imperative. Although these people may be grieving alongside you, they should become a pillar of light for you. Let them help to promote coping tools, like having someone to open up to. Sometimes, having someone in the room with you can be a comfort. The thing that is most important to you should be to know you aren't alone. That there is someone there to hold you up when you may not feel like holding you up anymore. It's okay to let people know that you need help. It's okay to reach out to people.

If you don't have someone to help you through this, please do not be afraid to seek professional help. Many times, we just need someone to talk to. Many programs may have little to no cost to join. You may have community programs that you can go to where you will meet people who are a lot like you or have the same feelings and issues.

JENNA'S STORY

Amidst the stormy fog that was Lisa's reality following the unexpected loss of her husband, a light of hope and strength emerged in her longtime friend, Jenna. The sudden hole left by her husband's departure is vast and disorienting. It is in these moments we need the presence of a true friend.

Jenna stepped up and met Lisa's grief with a quiet and steadfast determination. She did not attempt to fill the silence with meaningless platitudes nor trivialize the depth of Lisa's sorrow and pain. Instead, Jenna was just there. She was there to sort all things legal, the planning of the funeral, and the challenges Lisa faced each day waking up into this nightmare. Jenna stepped in to make sure Lisa never had to face these tasks alone but chose to be with her every step of the way.

Jenna's support came in many forms. She would take Lisa on walks in nearby parks, go to the beach and watch the sunset, and sit on the porch in the evening to enjoy just being there. Jenna didn't want to distract Lisa from her pain but to remind her that there was a world outside of those feelings, and that the continuity of life could bring about finding joy in life again. The bond between these ladies grew closer and deepened with each day. When Jenna showed unwavering support to Lisa and acted as a testament to the resilience of human connection, she became the beacon Lisa needed to move forward. Lisa felt that while the love she had lost would never be replaced, the love she had surrounding her was undeniable, boundless, and unyielding.

Amid one of life's harshest times, Jenna showed Lisa that while grief is a journey, you must ultimately navigate it personally, and having a compassionate friend by one's side tends to make the path a little more bearable.

So, as we see, human compassion is definitely essential to a grieving spouse. And every act of kindness can be the determining factor to make that person see the goodness in going on.

As we close this chapter, one thing is obvious. Grief is different for each person who goes through it. The manifestation can be one of many beasts in various forms. It is complex and multifaceted. There isn't a manual that says how each step should be and just how long this process will take you. But, understanding the significance of emotions and physical presence and seeking support seems to make the path more navigable.

The weight of grief is undeniable. Understanding its many facets becomes our guide day to day. In the next chapter, we will dive deeper into sorrow and ways to navigate as it twists and turns and how it shapes our daily lives.

2

RIDING THE TIDAL WAVE: THE STAGES OF GRIEF

"You are everywhere I look, but the pain of your loss is everywhere too."

Much like the ceaseless tidal waves of the ocean, grief has a rhythm of its own. The way it comes crashing down upon us, then pulling back and surging forward. It is as unpredictable as it is powerful. To navigate through the depths of grief, it is essential to understand its stages and the nuances that make each person's experience unique.

To understand these stages, let's look at Elisabeth Kubler-Ross, a pioneering psychiatrist, who introduced the five stages of grief and originally formulated it to understand the process patients go through as they deal with terminal illness. However, these stages have been widened to encompass the bereavement process broadly.

STAGE 1- DENIAL

Many times, this phase acts as a defense mechanism. It is our first defense against the torrent of pain we are not yet ready to face. It can help numb us to shocking news, making reality seem more bearable. Denial gives us the chance to pace our feelings of grief, allowing us only to accept what we can handle at that time. This often happens at the onset of the news of a passing so that we can wrap our heads around it. For example, Jane received the news of her brother's sudden death in a car accident, and her immediate reaction was disbelief. "There must be some mistake," she murmured repeatedly, hoping the next phone call would confirm her suspicion that it was a terrible mix-up. She went about her day, almost mechanically, holding onto the notion that everything was as it should be. It wasn't until she walked into her brother's room, seeing his unworn shoes and unread books, that the weight of reality began to descend. In its ultimate embrace, denial gave Jane a brief respite before the full force of her grief could take hold of her.

STAGE 2 – ANGER

As the masking effects of denial fade, the pain re-emerges, and to deal with it, we often display anger. This anger can be directed towards many different things and in many different ways. We can be angry at inanimate objects, strangers, friends, or deceased spouses. We understandably feel as though someone or something is to blame for our feeling this pain, even if it's not logical. At the time, it was logical to us. If you have this anger and cannot seem to move past it, a productive way to handle it may be to attend counseling or support groups. Sometimes, we need others to understand this feeling and how to negate it.

An example of the anger phase could be seeing an older couple walking together hand in hand. You immediately feel angry towards this couple because you felt robbed of this part of your marriage. You don't know these people, and they may be wonderful people, but in your mind, they represent a feeling of something you lost.

As you can see, this is a challenging phase of the grief process. There are so many ways that grief can manifest, but you must try to remember why you feel the way you do and not let it take over your thought process.

STAGE 3 – BARGAINING

This stage is the nuanced stage in the grief process, and it often is a desperate attempt to negotiate away the pain and reality of a loss. When we face the enormity of what this loss is to us, we begin to reach out to a higher power, fate, or even the universe, seeking a way to exchange a way to relieve our pain or, sometimes, even reverse a loss. When you feel powerless, you need to regain control of your life.

One example of bargaining would be religious bargaining. As a person is praying, they promise to go to church more, be a better Christian, or make specific changes in their lives in exchange for the return of the person lost or for relief from the intense pain they are feeling.

Another example would be a regretful rumination. We often think, "If only we had gone to the doctor sooner," or "If I had been there, the outcome would have been different." These are wishes to go back in time and change the outcome. We know that we really can't, but it's a way we have of making those bargains.

While still another example of bargaining is to make personal promises. People may make deals within themselves, such as "I'll never get mad again if they can come back.", or "I promise I will completely dedicate my life to helping others if only this pain will lessen."

So, these are just a few examples of how we acknowledge our feelings—recognizing that bargaining is part of the grief process and is just showing your love and reflecting the depth of your pain.

Sometimes, it helps to open up to someone you can trust. Sharing these feelings can help us understand and see more clearly that your offer is unreachable or unrealizable. Someone may be able to help you understand that some of these promises are irrational. We need to hear it from the other side to help us realize that this isn't the best way to stop hurting, but it is just a phase we will make it through.

If you have a journal, write down your feelings and the bargains you are making. Sometimes, just seeing them on paper will help you with your perspective of what you are asking for.

You can use meditation, which can help ground you in the present. Helping to let go of "if only" ruminations and wishes to change the past. Meditation will allow us to see more clearly.

Stay connected with family and friends or support groups. It often helps to have others who may be feeling the same way you do, and it will help you understand your feelings.

As always mentioned, see professional counseling if you cannot get past these feelings. They may be able to give you coping strategies or help guide you through the complexities of your stage and how you are handling it.

Here is a short story of an example of the bargaining stage.

Sarah sat in the quiet of her room, surrounded by the many pictures of her husband, Mark. They had shared an incredible 30 years together. A sudden illness has taken him away from her. When saying her prayers, she would whisper, "If only I could go back and get a second opinion, maybe he would still be here."

She would wake up every morning and promise, "If you give him back to me, I'll volunteer at the hospital. I'll help others and be more present in the community." She negotiated with fate, willing to change everything about her life if only she could rewrite the past.

One evening, Sarah decided to attend a local grief support group. As she listened to the others, she realized that she wasn't the only one doing bargaining. One lady spoke of the way she was bargaining. She would make promises to be a better mother in exchange for her child back. Another gentleman in the room talked about his regrets and how he wished he could have changed his actions to prevent his wife's accident.

So, in hearing these shared stories, Sarah found strength. She found an understanding of what bargaining for what it really was. It reflects her deep love for her husband and the void his lack of presence caused. With time, guidance, and much support, Sarah learned how to navigate this stage of her grief process and find a way to move forward. In the process, she remembers the cherished memories of the time and life she shared with her husband.

STAGE 4 – DEPRESSION

Depression is one of the stages in the grieving process. It is a deep and introspective type of sadness. It's not just the sadness of loss but can also be the realization of the impact of that loss. This stage often accompanies feelings of emptiness or despair. It can have an overwhelming sense of longing for something that isn't there. The weight of this reality that the one you truly loved is gone presses on your emotions, and the person grieving may feel as though they are enveloped in a thick fog of sorrow.

We must distinguish between the depression stage and clinical depression. While they tend to share some symptoms, the depression stage of grief is a natural part of the mourning process. Clinical depression is a mental health disorder and will require different kinds of intervention.

Here are a few examples of the Depression Stage

Julia's Story

Julia lost her sister to cancer. In the months following her sister's death, she often found herself in her sister's room, unable to summon the energy to face the world outside. Days felt long and purposeless. Julia's friends took notice of the withdrawal and reached out to help. They began to visit regularly and ensure that she wasn't alone. As time passed, Julia began to find solace in art. She used painting as an outlet to express her feelings and eventually channeled those emotions into beautiful creations. She found peace amidst her pain through her art and friends' support.

David's Experience

After the sudden loss of his son, David became engulfed in grief and felt numb and even aimless. The home was filled with his memories, making it even harder for David to cope. David recognized that he needed to process and deal with his loss and his emotions. He decided to join a grief support group. This allowed him to share his feelings and listen to the stories of others. He began to feel less isolated, and it even gave him some perspective on his feelings. He realized the importance of seeking healing and started attending weekly sessions. Over time, the combination of group and individual therapy provided him with the tools and coping mechanisms he needed to navigate his intense emotions.

Janice's Journey

When Janice's long-time partner passed away, she felt a profound sense of loneliness and despair. She felt there was a question as to her meaning of life and the place she had in it. Her daughter got very concerned and decided to teach her mother about meditation and mindfulness practices. Rita didn't think this would help much but decided to go along with it for her daughter. As she learned more and delved deeper into meditation, she realized it gave her moments of respite from the anguish she was feeling. The act of grounding herself in the present and focusing on her breathing and the world around her provided a sanctuary of sorts from the overwhelming tide of sorrow. She began taking long nature walks and combined them with her new meditation process and found healing in the embrace of the natural world.

So, as you can see, there are many ways to cope with this stage of grief, and each person will have to find their own way. Here are some suggestions for you: seek support, engage in activities, avoid isolation, consider meditation and mindfulness, and accept your feelings.

In the journey of grief, the depression stage is undeniably challenging. Yet by doing these things listed, and with support, understanding, and time, you may find the path through sorrow and towards acceptance and healing.

STAGE 5 – ACCEPTANCE

This stage does not mean that the person is "okay" with the loss, but they have come to terms with the reality that their spouse is no longer with them. It's about realizing that life, although changed, will go on. The person starts to find ways to move forward and live a fulfilling life despite the emptiness.

Acceptance is often regarded as the "final stage" of the traditional model of grief. It doesn't signify the end of pain or a return to the state of being before the loss. What it does represent is a point of understanding that the loved one is no longer physically present and the realization that life has been irreversibly changed. And despite all of this, life can and will continue. It's the understanding of a new reality in which we will live.

In reaching the acceptance stage, many may find peace, not because the pain is still there or has vanished, but because we have integrated the loss into our lives. It's where, as individuals, we begin to reengage with the world and partake in activities, reconnect with friends, or seek out new experiences. The sharpness of the pain starts to become a softer and more sporadic feeling. The feeling is often replaced with a gentle nostalgia or fond memories of the person no longer there.

While acceptance may seem like the grieving process's conclusion, we must understand that grief is non-linear. Elisabeth

Kubler-Ross's stages provide a framework, but in reality, the grieving journey is personal and often unpredictable. People might find themselves oscillating between anger, denial, bargaining, and depression long after they have felt they reached acceptance. This ebb and flow is natural, and seemingly inconsequential triggers can reignite the feeling of loss, emphasizing the importance of recognizing grief as a dynamic, ever-evolving process rather than a static sequence of stages.

As you can see, grief, in its essence, is not a straight pathway with a clear beginning and a clear end. More likely, it resembles a winding road with peaks, valleys, and unexpected detours. Many individuals will revisit stages they believe they have already passed or experienced simultaneously. One may wake up in the morning in acceptance while feeling the pull of depression by noon and could be consumed by anger by the evening. Another day may blend the stages of bargaining and denial, characterized by a sincere hope that things could revert to the way they were. The stages don't come with timestamps; they can last moments, days, or years and indeed recur.

It's entirely possible and natural to feel the weight of several stages at once. The quiet sadness of depression may exist with the immense turmoil of anger. Bargaining can often interlace with denial, creating a complex tapestry of emotions. This multi-faceted nature of grief can be overwhelming and sometimes contradictory. However, acknowledging this complexity can be the first step towards understanding one's personal grieving process.

Here, we will share a story of Emma's rollercoaster of grief as an example.

Emma's world came crashing down when her brother, Ben, unexpectedly passed away. The initial shock had her in disbelief; she half expected Ben to walk through the door, laughing at the enormity of the situation. But as the days turned into weeks, the weight of his absence became undeniable. Anger consumed her: anger at the world, at Ben for leaving so soon, and at herself for lost opportunities to say everything she ever wanted to.

Months later, on a particularly gloomy evening, she bargained with the universe, promising to be kinder, more present, more "in the moment" if it meant one more conversation with him. She dove into a pool of sadness, often feeling like she was drowning in despair. Then, in its own time, acceptance dawned, bringing a semblance of peace.

However, Emma's journey didn't end there. A song on the radio, a shared memory, or even a familiar scent would hurl her back into the depths of grief, reigniting anger or plunging her into sadness. Recognizing these triggers became Emma's beacon. She began journaling, noting what evoked intense emotions, and sought therapy to develop coping mechanisms. Over time, she found solace in creating a memory box dedicated to Ben, filling it with items that celebrated their bond. Whenever a trigger emerged, she'd turn to this box, allowing herself to feel, reminisce, and heal a little at a time.

So, the key to navigating the non-linear path of grief is recognizing and understanding one's triggers. These triggers can unexpectedly reignite feelings of loss, thrusting an individual back into any of the grief stages. However, with awareness comes the power to cope. Over time, with support and personal reflection, individuals can learn to face these triggers, allowing themselves to feel the emotion fully and then using coping mechanisms, like journaling, therapy, memory boxes, or support groups, to regain their footing. The journey through grief is like a rollercoaster, but with understanding, resilience, and time, it is a journey one can navigate.

Just as every individual is unique, so is their journey through grief. The pain of loss is universal, but how one navigates that pain, processes it, and eventually finds a path forward is deeply personal. Grief is influenced by myriad factors: the nature of the loss, one's relationship with the departed, emotional coping mechanisms, cultural backgrounds, and even previous experiences with loss.

Society often imposes arbitrary timelines and "shoulds" on the grieving process. Phrases like, "It's been months, why are you still feeling this way?" can, unfortunately, be all too common. However, it's crucial to remember that grief doesn't abide by a calendar. For some, the acute pain of loss might diminish within months, while for others, it could take years. And for many, that pain may never entirely disappear. It simply evolves, taking on a different texture or resonance over time. Rejecting societal pressures means permitting oneself to mourn in your way, at your own pace.

While there are general coping mechanisms that have helped many in their grieving journey, such as therapy, support groups, or journaling, it's essential to find what genuinely resonates with you. Some might find solace in nature, others in art, while others may use spiritual practices or rituals to navigate pain. Remember, it's not about what you "should" do but what genuinely helps you heal.

Here are some stories about different cultures and their levels of expectations and acceptance.

Raj's Story – India

In India, Hindu morning practices have strict timelines and rituals, including the 13-day mourning period following a death. When Raj lost his wife, he was expected to abide by these customs, including daily rituals and receiving guests paying condolences. However, Raj felt the weight of expectations stifling. While he appreciated the community support, he felt the need for solitude, for quiet reflection away from societal norms. Balancing his personal needs with expectations became a challenging aspect of his grief.

Armina's Tale – Morocco

In many parts of Morocco, grieving women are expected to wear white to symbolize their mourning, avoiding bright colors and festivities. Amina, having lost her brother, felt these cultural expectations clashing with her internal coping mechanisms. For her, painting, often in bright and vivid hues, was therapeutic. The external expectation of subdued mourning was at odds with her vibrant expressions of grief and love for her brother on canvas.

Liam's Experience – Ireland

Ireland, with its deep-rooted Catholic traditions, has specific rituals for mourning, including wakes and funeral masses. Liam, having lost his partner, found himself caught between the traditional mourning practices of his community and his personal beliefs as a non-religious individual. While the community sought comfort in prayers and religious ceremonies, Liam grappled with finding his secular means of saying goodbye, honoring his partner's memory without the veil of religion.

So, although society may look at things one way, this is a personal journey for you. It would be best if you made it work the way you need it to in order to heal. The challenge of grieving, especially within specific cultural contexts, is the delicate balance between personal needs and societal or familial expectations. It's essential to remember that while traditions and rituals can offer solace to many, one's journey through grief is paramount. Navigating external expectations requires setting boundaries, seeking understanding, and, most importantly, self-compassion.

Your grief, like your fingerprint, is uniquely yours. In a world filled with "should" and timelines, remember to honor your feelings, respect your pace, and find the coping mechanisms that genuinely resonate with you. Embrace the uniqueness of your journey, granting yourself the grace to grieve in your way.

Highlighting that understanding one's emotions is only the first step. Moving forward requires a conscious effort.

3

REBUILDING FROM ASHES: FINDING PURPOSE AGAIN

"In an instant, it was like the lights were put out. I couldn't see or find my way until I remembered the light of your memory."

"From the ashes of devastation, resilience blooms, reminding us that even in our darkest moments, the strength of the human spirit can illuminate the path forward."

Throughout life, we undergo various transformations, both external and internal. Career shifts, relationships, health challenges, significant losses, or even transformative personal choices can profoundly influence our perception of self. These changes, especially when abrupt or unexpected, can cause our internal self-image to be misaligned with the external reality. It's like a disturbing feeling of expecting to see a younger version of ourselves in the reflection, only to be met with the undeniable signs of time.

With its profound and all-encompassing nature, grief has a unique way of reshaping our very essence. The self, as we know it in a world colored with the presence of our spouse, undergoes a metamorphosis, emerging as a composite of the past, present, and aspirations for the future. The Evolution of Self is a journey of introspection, growth, and renewed identity. This chapter delves deeper into this transformative voyage.

We begin by looking at the altered reflection—the reflection of us into me. When two lives intertwine, identities often merge. Aspects of both partners influence preferences, choices, and dreams. Post-loss, there is a rediscovery phase that includes:

Individual desires: Understand what YOU truly want, devoid of past compromises or shared aspirations.

Personal Growth: Pursue growth areas that might have been sidelined or undiscovered in the shared journey.

Celebrating Individuality: Embrace and cherish unique qualities and view them as strengths.

Next, we approach the power of your memory and constructing the self with past experiences. While you learn from the past, your shared journey was filled with lessons. Harness those lessons to shape the evolving self. While honoring the bond, you should understand that incorporating elements from the past does not mean you are stagnant, but it's a tribute to the bond shared and a foundation for a new self. You can be selective. It's okay to let go of memories that bring pain, focusing instead on those that empower and inspire.

When you have a loss, you may think the future looks bleak. But as the initial despair wanes, it offers a canvas of possibilities, so why shouldn't you paint a new canvas with the future? Allow yourself to dream and envision a future that might have seemed improbable or even impossible at an earlier stage of your life. Try some new skills. Take up new courses or hobbies. This helps you to enrich your soul and add layers to your evolving identity. And yes, there are risks, so without being reckless, take calculated risks. They will propel your growth and help you find self-discovery.

LET'S LOOK AT CLARA'S STORY.

Clara, once an accountant, had always played it safe. Her choices complemented her husband's adventurous spirit. His sudden passing felt like the snuffing out of all vibrancy in her life. However, as months rolled into years, Clara began channeling her grief into art. What started as a therapeutic doodling transformed into intricate paintings.

She soon found herself enrolling in an art class. Then, hosting an exhibition and eventually transitioned into a full-time artist. The paintings became a dialogue between her past and present, each stroke a testament to her evolving self, rooted in memories but reaching new horizons.

As you can see, the self can evolve. As well as relationships. Dynamics may be altered. As you change, relationships with family or friends might shift. Some become stronger as others tend to wane. But the evolved self attracts different people, leading to new friendships or even romantic relationships. So, keep open communications with those important to you, which will help with navigating the shifting sands.

The evolution of self is a deeply personal journey. It's an amalgamation of memories, current experiences, and future aspirations. It's a dance of the soul, moving between the realms of the past shadows and hopeful light, crafting an identity that's both an ode to the ancient and a ballad for the days to come. The path isn't devoid of thorns, but each step taken is a testament to resilience, love, and the indomitable human spirit.

Dissonance is the context of grief and personal transformation and refers to the tension or conflict within oneself stemming from contrasting beliefs, emotions, or values. This internal discord can manifest after losing a spouse, especially if individuals try to reconcile their past selves with their evolving identities. Grappling with dissonance is akin to balancing on a tightrope, striving for alignment amidst winds of change. We will delve deeper into understanding, managing, and eventually harmonizing this inner conflict.

Many times, we cling to the past. We hold tight to memories that can sometimes jar against the actual reality of the present, causing dissonance.

We find that nostalgia can be a double-edged sword. When we reminisce, it can provide us with solace, idealizing that the past can create an emotional chasm between then and now.

So, we must honor both selves. The version from the past and the evolving self. Both are integral to your identity, and both deserve respect and acknowledgment.

We make new choices, we have old regrets, and as we begin to chart a new life course, we will make choices that the previous "couple" version of oneself wouldn't have made, which can lead to doubt and guilt. This is a form of decisional dissonance. We begin to validate our choices. Every post-loss decision needs validation, not as a comparison to the past, but for its merit in the new context.

Learning from regrets is not what we want to do. Rather than allowing regrets to augment dissonance, use them as learning experiences to make better, more informed choices moving forward.

HERE WE HAVE A STORY OF SOPHIA'S GARDEN:

In her attempt to heal, Sophia decided to transform her backyard, which she had previously designed with her late husband,

Peter. But, with every new plant she introduced or old one she relocated, she felt a gnawing guilt. Was she erasing shared memories?

While sitting in her revamped garden one evening, a butterfly reminiscent of one Peter had loved settled beside her. It was a moment of epiphany. She wasn't erasing the past but blending it with the present, creating a space that honored them both.

So, from this story, you can see that there will be times when you question your decisions, and it's okay to do that.

You will have pressure to grieve or move on in what our societal norms call for, and this can sometimes cause or heighten inner conflicts. But have self-compassion over validation. Prioritizing self-compassion and individual timelines can mitigate the dissonance stemming from external expectations.

Lean on a trusted friend, loved one, or therapist to provide balanced feedback without imposing societal templates.

Grappling with dissonance, while challenging, is an integral part of the healing journey. It underscores the profound impact of loss and the tenacity of the human spirit to rebuild amidst turmoil. By recognizing, understanding, and eventually harmonizing this dissonance, one not only inches closer to healing but also cultivates a richer, multifaceted self-that's a beautiful blend of memories, present realities, and future hopes.

The profound pain of losing a spouse can often become a crucible, altering the essence of one's identity. This unsettling transformation is also an invitation to embrace a changed self. We are looking into the intricacies of recognizing, understanding, and wholeheartedly accepting this newly formed identity after the heart-wrenching loss of a partner.

So, a shift in perspective is from duo to solo. While a significant portion of identity was carved in tandem with a spouse, there's now a pressing need to discern what individuality means in their absence. We must explore how to be alone, not lonely. Being alone post-loss doesn't necessarily equate to loneliness. It can feel that way, but we are now moving forward. It's a space for self-reflection, growth, and empowerment. We have unique qualities that were once shadowed by the partnership dynamics and can now be brought to light and celebrated. And this isn't to say that your partnership crushed your personality in any way, just a way to say that now we must thrive as individuals.

Now, we have layers of transformation—a new multifaceted self. We know we will always have a grief imprint, and while painful, it enriches one's emotional spectrum, instilling a more profound empathy and understanding of life's fragilities. As we heal, we discover new interests. We often stumble upon previously unexplored passions or rekindle dormant ones throughout this quest. We look at the world in a different view. Moving forward isn't betrayal, but embracing the changed self is a tribute to the past and a commitment to the future.

We must introduce our new self. With change comes the task of presenting our transformed identity to friends, family, and society. Not everyone will accept the changed self, and that is okay. It is essential to stay true to one's own journey. Just be ready to face misunderstandings.

Seek support by engaging in groups or therapy sessions that will resonate with the experiences of your loss and your transformation.

Embracing the changed self after the loss of a spouse is a journey riddled with complex emotions, from profound sorrow to quiet hope. It demands courage, patience, and a lot of self-love. While the echoes of the past will always linger, they merge into the present melodies to compose a symphony of resilience, growth, and continued love. The changed self is a testament to the enduring spirit of humanity, showcasing the ability to find light even amidst the darkest storms.

Often, when we confront the change in our reflection, the reflection is less about the change itself but more about our perspective towards it. Instead of seeing loss, can we see evolution? Can we cherish what's been gained instead of focusing on what's gone?

Our reflections, while they carry the imprints of time and experience, also hold the promise of the future. They are a canvas of possibilities, waiting for the next chapter to be written.

Confronting a changed reflection is undeniably challenging. It's a journey through acceptance, understanding, and reinvention. However, by embracing our evolving selves, recognizing the power of perspective, and cherishing the richness of our experiences, we can find harmony between our internal self-image and the reflection staring back at us. In this dance of self-discovery, we learn that our true identity isn't static but is a beautiful, ever-evolving tapestry of life's myriad experiences.

So, now that we have accepted our new self let's look at some of the things we need to do to continue moving forward from here.

Life can sweep us into its currents, often leading us further away from our true passions and interests. Priorities shift, roles change, and while juggling responsibilities and navigating the challenges of our lives, our passions sometimes get shelved.

In the intricate dance of shared life, passions, once vibrant, can sometimes fade into the background. With the heartrending departure of a spouse, the canvas of existence, though initially marred with grief, offers an unforeseen space. The following sections will unravel the journey of rekindling passions once overshadowed, understanding the transformative power of love, and the delicate steps toward reconnecting with one's most authentic desires.

Passions aren't just hobbies; they're gateways to our true selves, our happiest memories, and our purest form of expression. When nurtured, they can provide solace, offer a sense of purpose, and become instrumental in the healing process. Taking up a once-loved activity can not only distract us from our grief but also as a bridge to happier times. This helps anchor our emotions and provide a sense of continuity in a world that might suddenly feel disjointed.

Specific passions might have been side-stepped for shared dreams or practicalities in compromises and marriage adjust-ments. Even in their dormancy, these passions often echo in moments of solitude, waiting for acknowledgment. And while grief can be consuming, it also unravels layers of the self, unearthing buried dreams and aspirations.

To nurture neglected passions, one must first create mental and physical space. This means decluttering schedules, setting aside dedicated time, and consciously committing. But beyond the logistics, it's also about permitting oneself. There's a guilt that sometimes accompanies pleasure, especially after a loss. "How can I enjoy this when they're gone?" However, it's essential to understand that rediscovering joy isn't a betrayal of memory but an homage to life and its innate capacity to renew.

Engaging in a cherished activity can be therapeutic, allowing emotions to flow freely. So, it can be seen as a cathartic release. While in the stormy seas of grief, passions act as anchors, providing a sense of purpose and direction. Reengaging will give you a chance to rebuild your identity. As one reconnects with lost passions, a renewed sense of identity begins to take shape, weaving together fragments of the past and present.

So how do I make space for this reconnection, you ask? Embrace solitude. Introspection in quiet moments can illuminate long-forgotten desires. You can honor memories. Recollect memories when this passion brought you joy and recognize their worth in the healing journey. And again, engaging in personal passions isn't a deviation from mourning but a tribute to life's multifaceted experiences.

Take that first step and venture into the known yet unknown. The journey to reignite passion doesn't necessitate grand gestures. A simple action, like picking up an old instrument or sketching a random doodle, can spark the trip. When you begin, you may be rusty, and that's okay. It might feel awkward or unpolished. It's vital to embrace the imperfections and savor the joy of reconnection. Sharing your journey with supportive friends and family or joining related communities can amplify motivation and provide valuable feedback.

The loss of a spouse, with its profound grief, paradoxically offers a rare window of introspection and rediscovery. With its unpredictable twists, life often presents challenges that can leave us feeling unmoored. Yet, within us lies the potential to heal, rediscover, and thrive. We honor our true selves by rekindling lost passions and paving the way for a renewed sense of purpose. While the void left by loss can never be entirely filled, passions have a unique way of weaving joy, solace, and hope into the tapestry we call life, guiding our hearts toward healing and transformation.

We have covered many things; we must begin by reassessing life goals and reestablishing independence.

You and your partner had dreams that you shared. Dreams you conceived together, mutual aspirations, and shared life goals now suddenly seem unattainable or irrelevant. Yet, as the fog of grief clears and gradually lifts, the horizon beckons with a possible new sense of purpose.

Every relationship is a tapestry of combined dreams, shared goals, and mutual aspirations. These objectives might revolve around career growth, financial stability, raising children, or growing old together. With the demise of a spouse, this tapestry seems to be torn, leaving one with disjointed threads of what was once a beautifully integrated design. The task then becomes twofold. How do I untangle these threads and weave a new pattern?

We must go through a process of discovery. Before charting a new course, we must reflect on our previous goals. Which were primarily yours? Which were your partners? And which ones were genuinely shared?

Prioritizing would be the next step. Recognize that it's acceptable to let go of specific shared aspirations that no longer resonate with you. However, identify the ones you want to pursue despite your partners' absence. Remember, continuing a shared dream can also be a way to honor their memory.

When you decide what you want to continue or start, seek outside advice or suggestions. Talk to your friends, family, or professionals who can offer a fresh perspective or help in reshaping particular aspirations.

Begin to set tangible objectives. While broad goals give direction, tangible objectives make the journey actionable. For instance, if a shared dream was to travel the world, perhaps it starts with a single trip you always wished to take. So, baby steps, as they say. Take a small bite instead of taking off too much at a time. Don't try and do it all today. There is time. And I know that time is much more precious after the loss of a partner, but don't get ahead of yourself.

It would be best if you reestablished your independence. You will begin to chart a solo course. You may find it challenging and liberating in its task of reestablishing independence.

Begin by looking at your finances. It would be best if you reassessed your finances. Consult a financial advisor to understand assets, liabilities and how to navigate your financial future. This is a crucial time to know what you have and will be doing with it.

The financial support that you once received from your spouse will not be available, so you need to find someone to help you or support your decisions. Seek a close friend or family member to help with the financial part of the support. Have someone to bounce your ideas off because you are still emotional and will need someone to help you make sound, clear decisions.

As discussed previously, revisit hobbies or passions that may have taken a backseat. This fosters your independence and fills your life with joy and purpose.

Build a support system. While trying to process and grieve, there will be many things you need to question and understand. Cultivate relationships with friends and family. Being independent doesn't mean being alone. It's about having the autonomy to choose your support.

The journey of reassessing life goals and reestablishing independence after the loss of a spouse is undoubtedly challenging. It's a dance between honoring the past and embracing the future. Yet, with reflection, support, and a commitment to oneself, it's possible to weave a tapestry that, while different from the original, is just as intricate, beautiful, and meaningful.

So, how do we embrace new routines? How do we start over? This task is daunting. And it is a significant part of healing. We are continually taking steps forward.

As humans, we thrive on routines. We expect a sense of order, predictability, and comfort. When you suffer a significant loss, practices that once brought solace can suddenly feel empty or painful, making the familiar seem alien. In these times, we must accept and embrace new routines. It's a transformative journey where we are creating new traditions, understanding that the past becomes memories, the refreshing allure of novel places, and the healing touch of giving back.

Traditions are the bedrock of our emotional lives. They serve as a link to our past, markers of time, and bridges to our future. While honoring old traditions is vital, creating new ones is also a profound strength.

They can serve as distractions initially. The purpose may be to fill time, but gradually, the traditions become significant in their own right. New traditions can be seen as an evolution, connecting the past, present, and future. You can forge new bonds and strengthen relationships by sharing or creating traditions with loved ones or friends.

When you are grieving, it often entails holding on to memories, but the balance is delicate between cherishing the past and becoming ensnared by it.

If you fixate on the past, you can prevent personal growth and hinder exploring new experiences. Holding on to old routines may unintentionally create barriers and keep supportive loved

ones away. It can be hard to appreciate the present if you look at an idealized version of the past.

Take a trip and experience some cultural diversion. Experiencing cultures and environments provides a broader view of life and its transient nature. When you have new places, you have distractions. Many places will demand unique stimulations, which will help you temporarily distract from your grief. Rejuvenate your surroundings. Nature, art, or simply a change in surroundings can invigorate the soul and offer moments of serenity.

HERE IS A STORY OF LINDA AND HER TRIP TO BALI.

When Linda lost Robert, her husband of 30 years, the walls of their home seemed to close in on her. Every corner echoed memories. On an impulse, she booked a trip to Bali, a destination neither of them had visited.

Bali offered Linda a haven with its serene beaches, intricate temples, and warm locals. She practiced yoga, learned a bit of the local dance, and immersed herself in the Balinese culture. One day, while watching the sunset, she realized she was laughing. A genuine, heartfelt laugh, something she hadn't done in months.

That trip didn't diminish her grief, but it allowed her a break from it, a moment to breathe, and a realization that joy could coexist with sorrow.

Remember to take care of yourself. Linda needed some time for her, and she took it. Don't be afraid to do the same. Take time for yourself.

The journey of grief is not about forgetting but evolving. Embracing new routines and traditions, venturing into unfamiliar places, and reaching out to others can pave the way for healing and rediscovery. While the past remains an integral part of the mosaic of life, the new pieces, however unexpected, bring vibrancy, depth, and a renewed sense of purpose.

I reflected on the inward journey so far, hinting at the external challenges and changes to come.

4

ALONE IN A CROWD: NAVIGATING LONELINESS

"The greatest tribute we can give the deceased is to keep living. For when we don't, we too shall die before our time."
–Charles Glasman

THE BALLROOM'S SILENT ECHO

The grand ballroom was aglow with golden lights, casting shadows that danced alongside the numerous guests who filled the space. Laughter echoed through the elegant archways, and the soft hum of conversations paired melodiously with the gentle notes of a piano playing in the corner. It was Elenor's sixtieth birthday, a milestone she once dreamt of celebrating with her beloved Samuel by her side. But with his sudden passing the year before, those dreams had taken on a different hue.

Elenor wore a deep blue gown, Samuel's favorite color on her, a tribute to his memory. He always commented to her how beautiful the color was with her eyes. She smiled to herself at this thought. Guests surrounded her, each one offering smiles, warm hugs, and hearty congratulations. Friends recounted tales from their youthful days, nephews and nieces playfully teased about her age, and her children gave speeches filled with love and admiration. And although all of this was happening around her, including her, she still felt somewhat alone, even though the room was packed, brimming with love for Elenor.

Yet, Elenor felt an island of solitude amidst the sea of faces. Each smile she returned, every laugh she shared, felt like she was watching herself from afar. Despite its vivacity, the ballroom echoed with a silence only she could hear. It was the absence of Samuel's whispered jokes in her ear, the lack of his hand holding hers, grounding her in moments of overwhelming emotion. Even surrounded by every loved one she could ask for, the void he left was all too palpable.

As the evening wore on, Elenor stepped onto the balcony, seeking a breath of fresh air—just a moment to be alone with her thoughts. Shortly after stepping outside, her granddaughter, Lucy, soon joined her. Without a word, Lucy wrapped an arm around her grandmother, resting her head on Elenor's shoulder. The two gazed out into the night, finding solace in shared silence. At that moment, Elenor realized that sometimes, words weren't needed. Some voids were too vast to be filled, but they could be acknowledged, and in that acknowledgment, there was comfort.

Losing a spouse is an agonizing, profound experience. One that you don't understand until you have to go through it. You are walking along together, and suddenly, half of a shared existence is absent, and the world can seem overwhelmingly large and empty. When dealing with a loss of this nature, the bereaved often find themselves on a precipice of two similar yet distinct emotions: solitude and loneliness. Though these feelings tend to cross over one another and blend, particularly in the haze of grief, understanding the distinction between the two can offer clarity and often help in the healing journey.

Solitude in the *Webster's Dictionary of the English Language* is - the state or situation of being alone. And in its purest form, it is a state of being alone. It can be intentional. It can be a moment or period when we can process our thoughts, navigate our emotions, and find peace within ourselves, even if it is only momentarily embraced.

Solitude can be seen as a therapy of sorts when following the loss of a spouse. You need these solitude times to think of shared memories, laughter, pain, regrets, and what-ifs; all demand reflection. The freedom to mourn in our way without society's watchful eyes, speak to the departed without words and reconnect with oneself outside the identity of being a partner.

Let's look at the nature of solitude for a grieving spouse and how we can use it to help us along our journey as needed.

Temporal Respite – Solitude offers grieving spouses a pause from the outer world, allowing them the space to journey through their landscape of memories. Within the moments of solitude, you have a retreat from society's expectations of "moving on," giving yourself the chance to embrace and process your grief at your own pace.

Intimate Conversations – As a widow, you may find yourself immersed in conversations with the departed. Although these conversations may be imagined, they can become therapy, offering a sense of continuity in the relationship, and helping to foster a connection beyond the physical realm.

Rediscovery of self – One of the things that grief can do is to overshadow identity. When in solitude, the widow can look directly at the void left behind and rediscover who they may be without their partner. This can pave the way for personal growth and understanding that self-reflection benefits that.

Encountering Vulnerability – Emotions become amplified when in solitude. You may face waves of vulnerability, sorrow, anger, and possibly even guilt. While seemingly daunting, meeting these emotions head-on can be cathartic, leading to deeper understanding and acceptance.

Artistic Impression – When channeling emotions, you may find solace in art. In many different forms, such as writing, painting, or music, solitude can be the nurturing environment to express grief and memorialize a loved one through art.

Spiritual Exploration – When you lose a partner, it may cause you to have existential contemplations. In solitude, you may realize that spiritual and philosophical questions and seeking the answers to these questions may give you solace in higher beliefs or meditative practices.

Nature's Embrace – Humans often look to nature for solitude. Ocean waves rolling and crashing on the beach, the quiet surroundings of a forest, or just looking up at the vastness of a starry sky can provide you with perspective and a sense of connection to something larger than yourself.

The Loneliness Dance – Empowerment can be found in solitude but can accentuate feelings of loneliness. Recognizing and addressing this duality is imperative, reminding us of the importance of balance. When to seek solitude versus when to reach out for human connections.

Legacy Building -When quiet, our mind allows us to contemplate our legacy. We reflect on how we should honor our partner's memory. We consider things such as charitable acts, storytelling, passing along traditions and values, or all the above.

Gateway to resilience – Every moment of solitude in which we find ourselves can be a step towards stability. Although the void remains, the strength we garner from introspective solitude can help a grieving spouse find the courage to face another day, cherish the memories, and embrace future possibilities.

So, while the journey through grief is intensely personal, understanding the myriad of ways in which solitude will interact with our process can provide clarity and direction during the most challenging of times.

We will now look at loneliness. Loneliness is defined as being alone or isolated. So, on the other hand, we see that loneliness isn't always a choice. It's an emotional state marked by isolation, even when surrounded by others.

The profound loss of a spouse transforms loneliness from a fleeting feeling into an omnipresent companion. In the quiet moments after the condolences have faded and life has ostensibly moved on for the world, a lingering emptiness remains for the bereaved.

When a spouse departs from life, their presence still lingers in the silence, the empty chair across the dinner table, the vacant spot on the other side of the bed. This ever-present void can birth intense loneliness. The heart yearns for one more conversation, shared sunrise, and embrace. And in the vastness of yearning, even a room filled with loved ones can feel empty.

Yet, within this seemingly bleak expanse, there's an unspoken depth to embracing loneliness that is both poignant and transformative.

Embracing loneliness doesn't mean succumbing to despair; it's about acknowledging the profound absence and granting oneself the grace to grieve fully. In these solitary moments, one might hear the echo of shared laughter or see the ghost of a shared dance in the living room. Loneliness acts as a mirror, reflecting the depth and significance of the bond that once was. So, fully confront and embrace this solitude of sorts. Begin to form a sacred space where memories are honored and the departed spouse's spirit is kept alive. As time passes, you realize that this embrace has become a testament to love's enduring power, proving that even in the absence, the essence of your loved one continues to shape and influence the journey ahead.

As you can see, the line between solitude and loneliness is a journey of grief in which a spouse can often feel like they are walking on a tightrope, with solitude on one side and loneliness on the other. What begins as a moment of self-sought solitude can quickly become a cavern of loneliness. The subtleties distinguishing between these two states are profound, and understanding them can be pivotal in the healing process. Recognizing the transition is vital.

One should be aware of the duration and frequency of their moments of solitude. In its essence, it is a deliberate act. It's the conscious choice to be alone, allowing for introspection, reflection, and a deep engagement with one's emotions. For a grieving spouse, moments of solitude can be hallowed spaces where memories are replayed, love is remembered, and pain is processed without the interference of the outside world. Solitude offers the bereaved a controlled environment to relive moments, both bitter and sweet, and come to terms with the changing dynamics of their life. Regular check-ins with oneself, understanding the emotional state, and seeking a balance between solitude and social connection become imperative.

On the other hand, loneliness often feels like an unwelcome visitor, emphasizing the absence of a loved one and the stark void that remains. It is the yearning for a presence that is no longer there, a tactile reminder of loss, and a deep-seated sense of isolation. Loneliness can seep in uninvited, during social gatherings, where the spouse's absence is painfully felt, or in the middle of the night when the other side of the bed remains cold.

Loneliness, though painful, isn't devoid of value. It's a testament to the depth of connection shared with the departed spouse. Recognizing this can transform your loneliness from a mere aching void to a homage space to the loved shared.

Navigating the line between these states requires self-awareness and compassion. Recognizing when solitude is turning into loneliness is crucial. While solitude can be a sanctuary for healing, prolonged isolation and the accompanying loneliness can have detrimental effects on mental and emotional well-being. Thus, the grieving spouse needs to be vigilant about their needs: harness the restorative power of solitude and seek connection, support, and companionship when loneliness beckons.

Creating rituals can be beneficial in this journey. For example, designating specific times for solitude, like visiting a special place with memories or writing in a journal, can provide structure. Ensuring regular interactions with friends and family, joining support groups, or engaging in community activities can act as a buffer against overwhelming loneliness.

With time, patience, and understanding, it's possible to find a harmonious balance, honoring the memory of a loved one while slowly paving a path toward healing and rediscovery.

So, seek the gift of solitude. The serenity found in isolation can become a source of strength. Setting aside intentional moments for reflection, meditation, or simply being with one's thoughts can provide clarity and emotional release. Over time, these moments can become sanctuaries of healing and rejuvenation.

So, our conclusion is that the journey through grief, marked by solitude and loneliness, is deeply personal and varied. While solitude offers a serene space for introspection, loneliness underscores the depth of the bond lost. Embracing both, with understanding and self-compassion, can illuminate the path to healing. As the bereaved tread this path, they will discover that even in the quietest moments of solitude or the deepest pits of loneliness, the love shared with their departed continues to echo, offering solace and strength.

The fabric of a shared life with a spouse is intricately woven with numerous moments, milestones, and memories. You have journeyed together through celebrations, challenges, and countless everyday joys and sorrows. The loss of your partner leaves behind an emptiness that makes approaching life's milestones without them feels like trying to dance with a missing beat. However, as you continue to navigate the landscape of life, it's essential to embrace these milestones and events, albeit with a heart that remembers and sometimes aches.

Birthdays, anniversaries, holidays, and life's significant events all carry an inherent weight after the loss of a spouse. What were once occasions of joy and camaraderie can now stir up an amalgam of emotions: the joy of the day juxtaposed with the ache of absence. The place where they once stood, whether by your side cheering the loudest or offering a comforting hand during challenges, remains conspicuously vacant.

Yet, we must recognize that these milestones and events are still and always will be markers of our life's journey. They represent growth, time, resilience, and memories. And although you no longer have your spouse's physical presence, their essence continues to be part of these moments.

The first step in embracing these events in your life without your partner is to shift focus from their absence to homage. Instead of dwelling on the void, consider incorporating their memory into the occasions. On birthdays, maybe light a candle for them, or share a favorite story about them, or play their favorite song, or even have their favorite drink. It's all about celebrating their enduring presence in your life, even though the physical presence is missing.

So, you can honor past traditions, and it is comforting. Creating new ones can also be a part of the healing process. This doesn't mean you are leaving the memories behind of your partner, but instead, you are allowing yourself to evolve and find new experiences. These changes could be as simple as writing a letter to your departed partner on significant days, taking a trip to a place they always wanted to visit, or adopting a hobby they loved. The essence lies in creating new memories while carrying forward the legacy of the old ones.

As you navigate these milestones, leaning on others for support is okay. Surrounding yourself with people you love or those who understand your grief can offer immense solace. They can help you celebrate in a manner that feels right, providing a shoulder to cry on or simply sitting in silence, acknowledging the weight of the moment.

Even with a heavy heart, it showcases the strength and unsurpassable human spirit's ability to persevere.

The journey is painful, but there is a silent power in moving forward, carrying the torch of shared memories.

Loneliness isn't just about missing one person; it's about adjusting to an entirely altered social dynamic.

Navigating the social realm after a significant life change, such as losing a spouse, can be challenging and daunting. The dynamics you once knew or felt comfortable within can suddenly shift, casting you into unchartered waters. Relearning social dynamics is complex, multi-faceted, and deeply personal. Yet, it's an essential journey to undertake, facilitating growth, healing, and renewed connections.

The first step in relearning social dynamics is recognizing and understanding changes. The world may seem different, not because it has transformed, but because your perspective has. Activities you once enjoyed might now evoke strong emotions. Gathering where you once felt at ease might suddenly feel overwhelming. Conversations can become labyrinths, where every turn might lead to memories, sadness, or an uncomfortable silence.

While the idea might seem intimidating, venturing out solo can be a significant step in relearning social cues and dynamics. Start with small outings, perhaps a visit to a local café' or a short walk in the park. Gradually increase your exposure, maybe attending a workshop or joining a club. Being solo allows you to observe, interact, and adjust without the pressure of having someone else by your side. It fosters independence and will enable you to engage or disengage as you feel comfortable.

Often in social circles, especially as a couple, individuals are unconsciously typecast into specific roles. You might have been the 'planner" of the group or the "listener." However, the loss of a partner can shift these dynamics. It's essential to be open to adopting new roles or revisiting ones you might have relinquished. Being flexible can lead to unexpected discoveries within yourself and how you relate to others.

While being in the circles you have always frequented is comfortable, you must explore new adventures and avenues. These recent events can be therapeutic. Joining groups or attending events where you are a stranger, and no one knows your past or your loss allows you to be defined not by your loss but by your current interests and personality. Whether it's a book club, a yoga class, a gym, a pottery workshop, or something you enjoy, these environments can provide a fresh slate, even if it is just momentary.

But, before you head out on these new paths and dive deep into the external social world, you must reconnect with your inner self. Allow yourself to set boundaries, recognize triggers, and establish your comfort zones. With this introspection, you will provide a strong foundation and make your social interactions more authentic and meaningful.

While broadening your circle, do not forget to nurture your deeper, meaningful connections. These types of relationships are a stability and can act as an anchor in helping you to understand the more turbulent times. When you are with close friends or family, have conversations where you can openly share your feelings, fears, and aspirations. These types of conversations are healing to you. They offer a space where you can be vulnerable, helping readjust and relearn social dynamics.

Have you heard people say, after losing a spouse, "I could not ever date again; it's a different world than when I met my spouse." Often, when someone has been married for 10, 20, 30 years, or more, they are very correct in that statement. But you cannot be afraid to take that leap. Yes, things will be different, and that is okay. Many do not get remarried because they are scared to put themselves out there. But love is something everyone wants in their lives, so again, take the first step and see what goes from there. And if you don't feel you can, that is okay too. The introspection that you are doing will help you to know if you are ready for this move or not.

Relearning social dynamics after a life-altering event is akin to recalibrating a compass. The cardinal points might remain the same, but the path you chart is new, filled with discoveries, challenges, and moments of enlightenment. Embracing this journey requires patience, resilience, and self-awareness. As time passes and you weave through the intricate dance of social interactions, you will find your rhythm that resonates with your renewed self, leading to fulfilling and healing connections.

Social dynamics are the steps we've learned by heart in the dance of life. Yet, the music changes sometimes, compelling us to adjust our rhythm and relearn the patterns. For Helen, a return to her hometown after years abroad was much like rediscovering an old tune with a different tempo. "In a Familiar Place Through New Eyes: Helen's Journey," we will wade the waters of Helen's reacquaintance with her past and witness the nuances and subtleties she now perceives in a setting once deemed mundane.

A FAMILIAR PLACE THROUGH NEW EYES: HELEN'S JOURNEY

Helen stood at the garden entrance, her fingers lightly brushing the iron gates. For almost twenty years, she and Mark had visited this haven together every other weekend. They would meander down the cobblestone paths, find a quiet beach, and let hours slip away as they talked about everything and nothing. Today, the weight of his absence pressed down on her, making the gates seem heavier than ever.

She had debated long and hard about coming here alone. But a year after Mark's passing, Helen wanted to reconnect with places that had defined their shared life. She believed doing so could redefine her relationship with these spaces and create fresh memories to blend with the old.

As she walked through the entrance, Helen tried to see the garden as just a visitor, not as Mark's wife. She felt the sun's warmth filtering through the trees and noticed the scent of roses wafting by. Children played by the fountain, their laughter echoing the carefree days of youth. Couples strolled hand in hand, lost in their world, just as she and Mark used to be.

Helen chose a path they had not frequented much, seeking a new perspective in the familiar setting. Along this path, she discovered a hidden alcove shielded by lilacs. As she settled onto the bench, the serenity of the spot struck her. She could hear the distant murmur of water and the harmonious melodies of birds. The beauty of the moment was overpowering, yet the loneliness was palpable.

She closed her eyes, taking a deep breath. The garden had always been their place, but it was hers today. As memories of Mark flooded her thoughts, she didn't push them away. Instead, she let herself remember, smile, and even shed a tear. It was therapeutic, a blend of pain and peace.

When she opened her eyes, an older woman was sitting beside her, sketching the garden's panorama. They exchanged smiles. The woman introduced herself as Clara and explained that she, too, had lost a partner years ago. The park had been their sanctuary, and she continued to visit, finding solace and inspiration for her art. Over shared stories and laughs, the two formed an unexpected bond, realizing the comforting power of shared experiences.

As the day waned, Helen rose to leave, thanking Clara for company. The elderly artist handed her a sketch, a simple drawing of the alcove with two women chatting, framed by lilacs. "A memory," she said, "of a new beginning." Helen was very thankful for the sketch. She thanked Clara for the drawing.

Exiting the garden, Helen felt lighter than when she entered. She realized that while places carry memories, they also hold the promise of fresh experiences. The garden, blending old and new, symbolized her journey. Helen understood that while she would always miss Mark, she could find new meanings, connections, and joys even in the most familiar places.

And so, with a renewed spirit and the sketch clutched close to her heart, Helen stepped into the world, ready to embrace her solo journey, cherishing the old while welcoming the new.

So, no matter how well-trodden, our environments can always surprise and enlighten us. Helen's voyage back to her roots redefined her understanding of home and reshaped her identity within that familiar space. Through her eyes, we've been reminded that perspective can transform any known terrain into a land of discovery and growth. Just as Helen reconciled her past with her present, we, too, can find renewed meaning in the places and relationships we knew best.

The identity of a couple, with its shared memories, experiences, and dreams, is indeed beautiful. However, stepping out of this collective identity and embracing individuality can be equally enriching when circumstances demand. It offers a canvas to paint a life unrestricted by another's hues, where every stroke reflects the individual's unique essence. The journey might be sprinkled with challenges, but at its core, it is a voyage towards self-love, independence, and boundless potential.

5

RELEARNING SOCIAL BONDS: LEARNING TO REACH OUT

"Life can change in the blink of an eye, but love is eternal."

SECOND CHANCES AT HEALING: JOHN'S JOURNEY

John started at the worn-out pamphlet in his hand: "Heartstrings – A Support Group for Widows and Widowers." It depicted two empty chairs facing a sunset. His wife, Lucy, had passed away six months ago, and the weight of her absence was overwhelming. He found the pamphlet tucked away in one of Lucy's books. Maybe she wanted him to see it, or perhaps it was fate.

The community center's hallway was filled with the chatter of various group meetings. John hesitated outside the door marked "Heartstrings." He could hear soft voices, laughter, and the clink of cups. Every step towards that front door felt like a betrayal of Lucy's memory. But he also knew he couldn't drown in his grief forever.

Taking a deep breath, John opened the door. The room was cozy, filled with soft lighting. People were scattered about, some in deep conversation while others enjoyed a quiet moment with their tea. A lady with silver hair and a gentle smile approached him.

"You must be new here," she said, extending her hand. "I'm Clara."

John hesitated and then replied, "John. This is my first time."

Clara nodded, understanding in her eyes. "The first step is always the hardest. But we're here for you."

She led John to a circle of chairs. As he sat, a man shared a story about his late wife and their love for dancing—another spoke of the songs he and his wife used to sing. The stories weren't just of loss but also of love and the memories that never fade.

When it was John's turn, he spoke of Lucy – her infectious laughter, her love for gardening, and their Sunday morning rituals. As he shared, tears flowed, but so did the weight that had been pressing on his chest.

After the meeting, Clara walked with John to the exit. "It never truly goes away," she said softly, "But with time and support, it becomes bearable."

John nodded. "Thank you, Clara. I think Lucy would have wanted me to be here.

As John walked out into the night, he realized that healing didn't mean forgetting. It meant remembering, sharing, and allowing himself to be surrounded by others who understood his pain. And perhaps, with time, he could help someone else take their first hesitant step too.

So, we do want to take that first step, and it may seem like it's one of the biggest and tallest we will ever try and step up, but remember, every step up is also a step forward.

The power of shared experience, especially in spousal loss, is often likened to losing a piece of oneself. It is an experience that reshapes the dynamic of a surviving partner. However, it can also provide an opportunity for the rediscovery of bonds and the cultivation of resilience in unique ways. The unique grief that emerges from such a loss is deeply personal, but therein lies an avenue of profound connection: the shared experience of loss.

The immediate aftermath of a spouse's passing van often draws families closer. Shared grief becomes a common thread, binding family members in mutual understanding and empathy. Children, siblings, and extended family members can offer unique perspectives on the departed, enabling collective mourning and celebration of the loved one's life.

REDISCOVERING FRIENDSHIPS:

Losing a spouse can change the dynamics of friendships. Some friends may not know how to approach the grieving person, or conversations might become uncomfortable or awkward. However, the shared loss experience can also provide an opportunity to rediscover and strengthen bonds. Friends who have experienced similar losses often find a new layer of their friendship—understanding each other's pain, often without the need for words. Shared memories of the departed, once painful to revisit, can become healing anecdotes, bringing solace and a reminder of life's fragility and beauty. The comfort of familiarity is often a balm during trying times. After the loss of a spouse, old friendships offer a bridge to times preceded by pain. These friends knew you before, shared memories with you and your spouse, and understand the depth of your relationship and loss. Their shared history can provide a comforting backdrop against the tumultuousness of the present, helping to serve as gentle reminders of your identity, separate from your spouse's union.

However, revisiting old friendships may also reveal changed dynamics. As you've evolved through your grief journey, so too might have your needs and boundaries. Embracing these changes, communicating openly, and setting new boundaries can reshape these friendships into healthier, more supportive friendships.

On the other hand, some of those friendships may fade away. And that is okay too. Some of your friends won't know what to say or how to look at you and what you are going through. Just as you must give yourself time to heal, they have lost a friend also and may need to heal in their way. So be patient with the people around you. You may feel like they are abandoning you when you need them the most, but that isn't always the case. They often need to understand their feelings and how this loss will affect their dynamics.

STORY OF LALANI

Lalani was leaving the funeral of her husband. They had been together for 38 years. It was a harrowing day, and she just wanted to go home and lock herself in a room and cry. As she was leaving, many friends and family hugged her and offered to do anything she needed, just call on them. She tried to smile at them and make it through this for a few more hours. She was whisked away to a dinner for the family at a church. Again, she had many friends who were there, hugged, and said if you need anything, just let us know. Lalani smiled through her tears. Just a little longer, she thought to herself.

When she was finally at home, she realized how quiet her house was without her husband there. This brought on a new river of tears, and she decided she would need to turn on some music to help the room's quietness. As she did this, she began to think about what she would need to adjust to this newfound life. For now, she was alone in this world. She knew she couldn't fix a pipe if it broke, or put up Christmas lights, or even if she felt like doing those things. Who could she call on to help with these types of things? As she thought about this, she thought about her and her husband's very social life. The parties on the weekends, camping with friends, going out of town with friends. All these types of things would now be different. Could she do it alone? Would she want to do these things with all of her married friends? She may feel like the odd man out.

So, she decided to wait for the calls and the invitations to start coming back. She knew it would be a while, but that was alright. She would need time to want to go back to doing these kinds of things. A month went by, then a few months, then a year, and Lalani realized she hadn't been invited to anything in the past year. She got a call occasionally from a friend making sure she was okay, but really, no social involvement. She called a couple of her closest friends to see if something was happening. As she spoke to one of her closest friends, she noticed a different tone when she asked what everyone had been doing. Kind of like she wanted to tell her, but she didn't want to tell her. After that call, Lalani decided to call a few other people. As she was calling, she discovered many activities she was not involved in had been happening. So, she asked herself why no one was calling her.

After many discussions by phone after that day, Lalani realized that people didn't know what to say to her or how to react around her. This seemed to be the most resounding reason people stopped calling her.

As you can see, many dynamics in your life will change. Friends may change, may come, or may go. Just learn to take things as they come and handle them in the best way possible. It will be a difficult path that you are on, and the twists and turns will happen, but in the end, you will see where that path will take you.

SHARING GRIEF: THE POWER OF REDISCOVERING BONDS

When you have suffered a loss, such as a spouse, and you can connect with others who have also suffered in this way, it can lead to intense bonds. Many times, those who have walked the same path can genuinely comprehend. These are the connections you want to grow beyond shared grief. These bonds can blossom into meaningful, long-lasting relationships founded on empathy, trust, and mutual support and continued with love and understanding.

ROLES OF SUPPORT GROUPS

The world of grief can sometimes feel isolating, making new friendships essential. Support Groups, Grief counseling sessions, or community activities can be avenues to meet people who understand your journey or introduce fresh perspectives. These new friendships, devoid of any past baggage, offer a blank canvas, allowing you to redefine your previous marital identity.

Support groups such as "Heartstrings" offer a place to feel safe and process your grief. The group processes by sharing stories, remembrances, and a genuine understanding of how others are feeling. You are in the presence of people who get it. Their path of grief may have been full of twists and turns, but they lead you to each other.

Being surrounded by others who understand the myriad of emotions – from anger to guilt, sadness to confusion- creates a comforting environment where individuals can grieve openly and honestly. Sharing stories, coping techniques, and memories becomes therapeutic, allowing members to move forward without feeling alone.

While no one can replace a lost spouse, friends can play a pivotal role in healing. They offer distractions during over-whelming moments, lend an ear when you need to reminisce, or provide a shoulder to cry on during particularly low periods.

Over time, shared moments of grief, understanding, and even-tual acceptance can cultivate a rich soil from which stronger friendships grow.

CASE STUDY: THE SUCCESS OF GROUP THERAPY IN TREATING GRIEF

Group therapy has long been a cornerstone of the world of mental health, offering a unique dynamic where individuals can share, connect, and heal collectively. This case study delves into the profound impact of group therapy on individuals processing grief after significant losses.

"Pathways to Healing" is a grief-centered group therapy program in Minneapolis. Founded in 2010, it offers an eight-week structured course for individuals grappling with various forms of loss, from spousal and familial to sudden tragedies.

Participants:

The case focuses on a group of ten individuals aged 28-65, all of whom lost a loved one within the last 12 months. The diverse group comprised five who lost spouses, three who lost children, and two who lost siblings.

Method:

The eight-week program followed a structured approach:

Week 1-2: Introduction and storytelling, allowing members to share their loss stories and initial feelings.

Week 3-4: Addressing personal grief, identifying stages, and understanding individual responses.

Week 5-6: Learning coping mechanisms, introducing mindfulness, journaling, and memory exercises.

Week 7-8: Reintegrating into life, setting personal goals, and establishing support networks.

Therapists employed techniques like active listening, role-playing, guided meditation, and art therapy throughout the program.

Findings:

Shared experiences amplified healing. Participants noted that being in an environment where everyone has faced loss made them feel less isolated. Listening to other's stories gave them perspective and allowed them to see their healing journey in a broader context.

The group setting provided a judgment-free zone where participants could express their grief without social pressure. This catharsis was instrumental in their healing process.

In building support systems, many participants formed close bonds during the therapy sessions, extending their support networks. These connections often persisted after the program, creating lifelong friendships founded on mutual understanding and empathy.

The progression of sharing stories to reintegrating into life provided a clear roadmap for participants, allowing them to see their journey in stages, making the process seem more achievable.

The therapists played a pivotal role in navigating group dynamics, ensuring everyone felt heard, and introducing coping mechanisms. Their expertise was invaluable in guiding the group through their shared journey.

So, in conclusion, the "Pathways to Healing" case underscores the transformative power of group therapy for individuals grappling with grief. The shared experiences, skilled facilitation, and structured approach offer a holistic healing pathway. While individual treatment has its merits, group therapy presents a collective healing experience that can be pivotal for those in the throes of grief.

THE IMPACT OF THERAPY

We have spoken about support groups and how they can be helpful in helping you move on and process your grief, but now, let's look at therapy.

Therapy provides a much more individualized approach to dealing with grief. It offers a confidential, non-judgmental space where they can truly express their deepest emotions, fears, and hopes. This structured environment, facilitated by trained professionals, ensures that the bereaved can unpack complex feelings without fear of misunderstanding or judgment. A therapist, equipped with knowledge and tools, provides targeted interventions, helping individuals to process their loss healthily rather than bottling emotions or succumbing to potentially harmful coping mechanisms.

A therapist can help to navigate the treacherous waters of grief, offering coping mechanisms tailored to the individual's needs. They can address underlying feelings, help set grieving milestones, and provide a structured healing process. Combined with the shared experiences from support groups, therapy can be instrumental in the journey toward acceptance and healing.

One of the most significant impacts of therapy is its ability to help grieving spouses identify and confront unresolved feelings. The sudden nature of some deaths may leave behind a whirlwind of regrets, unspoken words, or unfinished matters. Therapy aids in addressing these unresolved issues.

Moreover, therapy assists in the rebuilding process. With the loss of a partner, many spouses face an identity crisis, struggling to define themselves outside the context of the relationship. Through therapy, individuals embark on a journey of self-discovery, reclaiming their individuality, and charting out a future that integrates the memory of their spouse while allowing for personal growth and new experiences.

In essence, therapy's impact on a grieving spouse is transformative. It's a compassionate hand that guides the bereaved through the darkest tunnels of grief, ensuring they emerge resilient, understand their feelings, and are equipped to embrace the future with hope and purpose.

STRIKING A BALANCE

Finding a balance between the past and the future is a delicate dance. It requires self-awareness, patience, and an understanding that life, despite its trials, offers endless possibilities. While the past, with its shared memories, provides comfort and a sense of identity, the future beckons with promises of growth, new experiences, and fresh memories.

The journey after spousal loss is about harmonizing these two timelines- respectfully cherishing what was while bravely stepping into what can be. In this balance, one discovers resilience, hope, and the enduring power of the human spirit to find love and meaning, even after profound loss.

6

DINNER CONVERSATION: FROM REGRET TO RECONCILIATION

"It's heartbreaking to know I didn't get to say goodbye, but even if I had, my love for you would never feel finished."

The sun dipped below the horizon, casting a warm, amber glow over the dining room. A solitary candle flickered in the center of the table, casting dancing shadows on the walls. A woman, Sarah, sat alone, her fingers tracing the rim of her wine glass as she contemplated the empty chair across from her. Tonight was different. Tonight was about confronting her deepest regrets and seeking a path to reconciliation with herself and her past.

When we begin to face our regrets, it's like looking into the corners of our minds, where the ghosts of our past refuse to fade away. Our thoughts are haunted, and these thoughts color our choices. We can even let them dictate our future. Sarah has carried her regrets like a heavy burden, one she couldn't seem to shake. But tonight, she had decided it was time to face them head-on.

So, what exactly is regret? It is a universal emotion, a product of a complex web of choices and chances that make up our lives. It can be targeted by many things, such as missed opportunities, from words we have spoken or not spoken. Sarah's regret was deeply personal. She had lost her husband, John, to a sudden illness years ago, and in the wake of his death, she was consumed by guilt for not saying the things she wished she had said while he was alive.

As she stared at the empty chair, she began to speak. Her voice was trembling with emotion. "John, I wish I had told you how much I loved you every day. I wish I had held you closer, kissed you longer, and never let a moment go by without letting you know how much you meant to me." She said all the things that she wanted to say before he passed away but didn't know how to articulate them at the time.

When we confront our regrets, it is not about erasing the past. It's a balm for the wounds we have inflicted upon ourselves for our choices and those we didn't make. For Sarah, this meant accepting and understanding that she couldn't change the past but could choose to live differently in the present and future.

Grief often has a way of amplifying our regrets. In the case of losing a spouse, the realization that there will never be another chance to make amends or express love can be overwhelming. Sarah's journey to self-forgiveness began with an understanding that these regrets were a natural part of the grieving process. They reflect the deep love and connection she shared with John, but they need not define her.

Self-forgiveness is the key that unlocks the door to reconciliation with our past. It is a gift we can give ourselves, especially when navigating the tumultuous waters of grief. It is an acknowledgment that we are human, imperfect, and bound to make mistakes. Sarah had carried the weight of her unspoken words and her perceived failures as a spouse for too long. It was time for her to forgive herself, and this realization was a pivotal moment in her journey.

Forgiving oneself is not easy. It requires that we look at ourselves as only human and know we can make mistakes but learn from them as we take this journey.

Self-forgiveness is not a one-time event but a process. So, let's look at ways we can face the healing power of self-forgiveness.

First, we must acknowledge that imperfection. Self-forgiveness begins with recognizing that we are not infallible. We make choices and decisions based on the information, emotions, and circumstances available to us at the time.

Next, we should let go of our guilt. Guilt is a common emotion in grief but can be particularly burdensome when directed inward. We must consciously release the guilt for what is holding us down. Guilt will only prolong our suffering and grief. We must face this issue head-on.

We must begin to be self-compassionate. Self-forgiveness is an act of this. It involves treating oneself with the same kindness, understanding, and empathy that one would extend to a dear friend. Begin by speaking to yourself with gentleness and reassurance. Give yourself grace.

Instead of dwelling on regrets as missed opportunities, reframe them as a testament to the love you shared with your spouse. These regrets echoed a deep connection and the desire for more time together. In your new light, the regrets become a source of gratitude for the moments you did get to share.

So, release your past. Forgiveness, including self-forgiveness, requires a conscious decision to release the grip of the past. Learn to focus on the present moment and the opportunities for growth and healing. It understands that holding onto regrets will only prevent you from moving forward.

A DREAM VISITATION FROM A LOST SPOUSE

That night, Sarah lay in bed and had an extraordinary dream. She found herself in a garden bathed in soft moonlight, the scent of roses filling the air. And there, standing before her, was John, her lost spouse. He looked just as she remembered him, with a warm smile and eyes filled with love.

In the dream, they held each other and communicated without words. John's presence was reassuring, as if he could come to offer his forgiveness and to tell her that he had always known how much she loved him. It was a dream visitation that brought forth both tears of joy and sorrow. But it was also a powerful symbol of reconciliation.

Dreams can bridge the conscious and the subconscious, where our deepest emotions and desires manifest. For Sarah, this dream was a gift – a way for her to feel the presence of her lost spouse one last time to find the closure she needed.

As Sarah woke from her dream, she carried a newfound sense of peace. However, she knew that the journey to self-reconciliation was ongoing. To continue this path, she turned to meditation and mindfulness as tools to center herself and cultivate inner healing.

Meditation is a practice that invites us to pause, breathe, and turn inward. For Sarah, it became a sanctuary – a place where she could temporarily escape the whirlwind of her emotions and be present with herself.

By cultivating presence, meditation allowed Sarah to anchor herself in the present moment. Instead of being consumed by thoughts of the past or worries about the future, she learned to focus on her breath and the sensations in her body. This simple act of presence brought a sense of relief. While in meditation, Sarah discovered the power of observation without judgment. She could watch her thoughts and emotions rise like clouds, acknowledging them without feeling compelled to act on or suppress them.

To find calm in the chaos, and even amid intense grief, Sarah found that meditation could be a source of calm. It didn't eliminate her pain, but it provided moments of respite and a reminder that she could still access a sense of peace within herself. Through meditation, Sarah practiced the art of releasing and letting go. She learned she didn't have to hold onto every thought or emotion. Some could be acknowledged and then released, creating space for healing and acceptance.

As Sarah embarked on her journey of self-forgiveness and immersed herself in the practices of meditation and mindfulness, she discovered they were not just momentary respites from grief but powerful tools for healing.

So, during her healing, these things she found helped her and can also be used if you need them for recovery.

Integration of Grief: Meditation and mindfulness helped Sarah to integrate her grief into her life rather than trying to banish it. She realized that grief was not an enemy to be defeated but a companion on her journey.

Lightening of the Emotional Burden: The weight of guilt and regret slowly began to lift. Sarah felt a sense of relief and liberation as she released herself from the emotional shackles that had bound her.

Emotional Resilience: Over time, these practices cultivated emotional resilience. Sarah became better equipped to handle the intense waves of grief, knowing that she could always return to the calm within herself.

Reconnection with Self and Love: Grief often leads to disconnection from oneself. Meditation and mindfulness allowed Sarah to reconnect with her inner strength, wisdom, and resilience. And in doing so, she reconnected with her love for John. She realized her love for him transcended time and space and that it would continue to exist in her heart without the burden of regret.

Acceptance and Healing: The stillness cultivated through these practices created spaces for healing. It allowed Sarah to process her emotions, confront her regrets, and ultimately find solace amidst the storm of grief. It allowed her to accept the reality of John's absence while cherishing the memories of the love they had shared. As Sarah forgave herself, she found the courage to take steps toward rebuilding her life. The self-compassion she cultivated became the foundation for future growth and happiness.

As you can see, it is a long journey that is well worth it as you heal. I will share a list of things you can do to help yourself begin this healing process.

1. Write letters to your spouse. Express all the feelings and thoughts you are having. These letters will allow you to release your emotions and say things you wished you had said while they were here.

2. Seek Support by contacting a grief counselor or joining a support group for widows and widowers. Sharing your experience with others going through what you are going through will provide comfort and a sense of belonging.

3. Embrace self-compassion as a daily practice. Treat yourself with the same kindness and understanding that you would offer a friend facing similar regrets.

4. Make a conscious effort to create new memories and experiences that bring you joy and fulfillment. This will help to shift the focus from the past to the present and future.

5. Perform acts of love and kindness for not only yourself but for others. These goodwill gestures can help reconnect with your capacity for love and compassion.

6. In your newfound self-compassion and ability to forgive yourself, you may find that it will spill over to other relationships. You may become more patient, understanding, and forgiving with friends and family.

7. Learn to embrace the present fully. Find joy in simple pleasures and approach life with a newfound sense of gratitude.

8. Be open to love. Even if you feel you will never love again, as you reconcile with yourself, realize that your capacity for love is not limited. Open your heart to new possibilities and maybe even find love once more.

9. Inspire the people around you. Your friends and family will see the transformative power of self-reconciliation and may begin their journeys of healing and forgiveness.

Dinner conversations can be a powerful vehicle for introspection and transformation. Sarah's journey from regret to reconciliation, guided by self-forgiveness, dream visitations, meditation, and mindfulness, is a testament to the resilience of the human spirit.

Regrets need not define our lives; they can serve as catalysts for growth and healing. Sarah's journey reminds us that the path to self-reconciliation is profoundly personal. Still, it affects ripples far beyond ourselves, shaping how we navigate life's broader shifts and demands.

As the candle continued to flicker in the dining room, Sarah raised her glass to the empty chair across from her. "Thank you, John," she whispered, "For the love we shared, the lessons I've learned, and the person I am becoming. I'll carry your memory with me, but I'll also carry the hope and strength to embrace life's uncertainties and joys."

And with that, she took a sip of the wine, knowing her journey from regret to reconciliation was far from over, but she was on the right patch – a path illuminated by self-forgiveness, love, and the power of healing from within.

7

A WORLD REIMAGINED: ADJUSTING TO NEW ROLES AND ROUTINES

"People say it takes time to heal, but seeing everything change in a moment changes the way I see time. It's not a simple progression of one minute to the next. Some moments stretch out into the years."

Reshaping a life after a vital loss is like reassembling a jigsaw puzzle with one missing piece. The empty space left behind by that missing fragment is a constant reminder of what will and will not be. Yet, carefully arranging the remaining pieces is a tribute to the beauty within the incomplete picture. As we search for ways to fill the void, we may discover new details we hadn't noticed before, forging a path of resilience and adaptation, slowly reshaping the puzzle of our lives into a new, intricate masterpiece.

There is a challenge to becoming a self-reliant person. And so many things will play into your new roles and choices.

One of the things will be emotional upheaval, which is followed by the loss of a spouse and can be all-encompassing. Losing a spouse is a profoundly devastating experience, and the emotional turmoil that follows can be overwhelming. Grief can manifest in a myriad of ways, from deep sadness to anger, guilt, and even numbness. Each day can bring about a rollercoaster of emotions. You may wake up and feel good and like you are coming out the other side when suddenly, a song, a smell, or a memory can turn your whole day around. It is difficult to find that sense of normalcy. Coping with the loss of a life partner means contending with the emptiness that accompanies their absence, as well as the sudden disruption of shared dreams and plans that will now not come to fruition. The journey through grief is profoundly personal and can be marked by intense moments of sadness and loneliness as the bereaved spouse navigates the complex terrain of their emotions.

Another of the challenges can certainly be the financial complexity of the situation. For many couples, financial matters are intertwined, with each partner playing specific roles. Financial complexity adds another layer of stress to an already challenging situation. In many cases, spouses often handle different aspects of the household finances, and when one is suddenly gone, the surviving spouse may struggle to make sense of their financial situation. There may be unexpected debts, legal issues, or insurance claims to contend with. The loss of a second income can also result in financial strain, forcing the surviving spouse to reevaluate their financial priorities and make difficult decisions about their future. It is often difficult to find a starting point when faced with this situation.

When it comes to household responsibilities, once shared between partners, can become an overwhelming burden for the grieving spouse. Tasks once shared between spouses, such as cooking, cleaning, and home maintenance, now fall solely on the surviving partner's shoulders.

The home, which used to be a place of comfort and companionship, can become a constant reminder of the loss. Maintaining household chores and maintenance may feel like an impossible challenge amidst the emotional turmoil.

A story of mine finding myself in this situation is this. Monday and Thursday were days that the trash ran, and you had to have the trash out early on those days. I got up on a Monday morning and was going about my day when I realized there was a trash bag, and I had to take it to the road. I fell apart and just hit my knees and cried. It was not because I had to take out the trash but because it was just one of the many things I now had to do on my own.

So, these times may trigger you when something such as this comes up, and you have to learn to be strong and know that you can make this happen, and you can do it. One step at a time, whether it is the trash, cooking, cleaning, or whatever. Know that you will make it through this.

That brings us to loneliness. We have covered some of this in earlier chapters, so we won't spend a lot of time on this, but remember that this is one of the most pervasive challenges faced by those who have lost a spouse. It often results in profound feelings of loneliness and isolation. The void left by the absence of a life partner can be felt more acutely during moments of solitude. Friends and family may offer support, but the loneliness that accompanies the loss of a spouse is a unique and often isolating experience. It can be challenging to connect with others who have not experienced a similar loss, making the grieving spouse feel like an outsider in their social circles.

Navigating these challenges after the loss of a spouse is a daunting and deeply personal journey. It requires time, patience, and often the support of a compassionate community or professional help to help the bereaved spouse gradually find their way through the emotional turmoil, financial complexity, household responsibilities, and the pervasive feelings of loneliness and isolation that can follow such a profound loss.

THE NECESSITY OF BECOMING SELF-RELIANT

Becoming self-reliant is a challenge and a necessity for personal growth and empowerment. The necessity cannot be overstated. When you suddenly find yourself alone, and you are thrust into a situation where you must take on responsibilities and decisions they may have shared previously. This newfound independence is crucial for their ability to navigate the challenges that follow. It is a journey of self-discovery, where you learn to rely on your judgement, adapt to a changed reality, and find the inner strength to rebuild your life. Self-resilience becomes the cornerstone of you building your future. It is an opportunity to discover your inner strength and resourcefulness, proving that you can navigate life's challenges independently.

Independence and empowerment are the natural by-products of this process. As the bereaved individual learns to make significant and small choices, they regain control over their life. This newfound autonomy empowers them to set goals, embrace opportunities, and pursue personal passions with renewed purpose. It's a journey of self-empowerment that can lead to a profound transformation and a rediscovery of one's capabilities.

Developing financial self-reliance is crucial. Financial stability is a critical aspect of this journey. It ensures you control your financial well-being and can make informed decisions about investments, retirement planning, and estate management. With the loss of a spouse often comes a significant shift in the financial landscape. The surviving spouse may grapple with complex financial matters they once shared. Achieving financial stability may require careful budgeting, seeking professional guidance, and making strategic decisions about investments and assets. Financial stability provides the security needed to face the future with confidence.

When we embrace self-reliance, it fosters adaptability. Adaptability is equally essential. Unexpected changes and challenges mark life after the loss of a spouse. It allows you to adapt to changes in your circumstances and take charge of your future. The bereaved spouse should be open to new experiences and willing to adjust to a different lifestyle. This adaptability can be a valuable asset in various aspects of life. Being adaptable also allows them to overcome obstacles and find solutions to the unique challenges they encounter along the way.

Becoming self-reliant doesn't mean facing grief alone, but it does mean building emotional resilience. Emotional resilience is the bedrock of this entire journey. Grief, loneliness, and emotional turmoil are natural companions after the loss of a spouse. Developing emotional resilience means acknowledging and processing these emotions while finding healthy coping methods. It involves seeking support from friends, family, or professionals, practicing self-care, and gradually healing from the profound loss. Emotional resilience enables the individual to survive and ultimately thrive, finding strength and hope in the face of adversity as they build a new, fulfilling life. Learning to cope with emotions and seeking support when needed are integral parts of this process.

STRATEGIES FOR DEVELOPING SELF-RELIANCE

1. Seek Professional Guidance – Engage the services of professionals such as financial advisors, attorneys, and therapists to provide expertise and guidance in their respective fields. They can help you navigate complex financial, legal, and emotional challenges.
2. Build a support network – Lean on friends and family for emotional support. Share your feelings, fears, and uncertainties with those you trust. Join support groups or seek counseling to connect with others who have experienced similar losses.
3. Organize and Plan – Create a detailed plan for our financial, legal, and household responsibilities. Organize important documents, such as wills, insurance policies, and financial records. Having a clear plan in place can alleviate stress.
4. Develop New Skills – Consider acquiring new skills your spouse previously handled. This might include learning essential home maintenance, budgeting, or even cooking if it wasn't your primary responsibility before.
5. Embrace Self-Care – Prioritize self-care to maintain physical and emotional well-being. Exercise, eat healthy, and get adequate rest. Engage in activities that bring you joy and provide a respite from self-resilience challenges.
6. Set Realistic Goals – Set achievable goals for your personal and financial future. These goals can serve as

motivating milestones as you embrace your new role as a self-reliant individual.

Becoming self-reliant after losing a spouse is a challenging journey that demands strength, adaptability, and resilience. While the emotional turbulence and practical complexities may seem impossible, we must not negate the importance of self-reliance.

This process is not about severing connections or forgetting your spouse but honoring their memory by living a fulfilling, self-reliant life. As you navigate the challenges and embrace your newfound independence, you will discover a profound sense of empowerment and the realization that you have the inner strength to forge a path forward, even in the face of loss. Self-reliance becomes a necessity and a testament to your capacity for growth and resilience in the face of life's most challenging trials.

ADDRESSING PRACTICAL LIFE ADJUSTMENTS

Since losing a spouse is profoundly challenging, we want to address some practical dimensions. Managing practical life adjustments can seem overwhelming, but they are essential to rebuilding and moving forward. We now explore the practical aspects that must be addressed after a spouse passes and offer guidance on navigating them with care and resilience. The following is a list of things as a kind of checklist to help you prioritize and remember things that may slip your mind at such an overwhelming time in your life.

1. *Financial Reassessment*

Financial stability is one of the most immediate practical concerns after losing a spouse. The household income may change, so reassessing your financial situation is crucial. Here are some steps to consider:

Review Finances – Take stock of your joint and individual financial accounts, including bank accounts, investments, and retirement funds. Consider seeking the advice of a financial advisor if necessary.

Update Beneficiaries – Ensure your spouse's life insurance policies, retirement accounts, and other assets have updated beneficiaries.

Budget Adjustment – Create a new budget based on your current financial situation. Adjusting your spending and saving habits may be necessary.

Debt Management – Address any shared debts or loans. It may be necessary to refinance or restructure them.

2. *Legal Matters*

The legal aspects of your life may require attention as well. Consult with an attorney to guide you through the processes. You may need to update legal documents such as wills, trusts, and powers of attorney to reflect your current wishes and circumstances. If your partner has an estate plan, it's essential to understand how it affects you and take legal steps to manage their assets and settle their affairs.

Estate Settlement – If your spouse had a will, work with an attorney to guide you through settling their estate, including the distribution of assets and addressing any outstanding debts.

Property Ownership – Clarify the ownership status of jointly-held property or assets. You may need to transfer ownership titles or update deeds.

Power of Attorney – Consider updating your power of attorney, healthcare proxy, and will to reflect your new circumstances.

3. Social Security and Benefits

Navigating the complexities of Social Security is another crucial step. Surviving spouses may be eligible for survivor benefits, including Social Security survivor benefits, pension plans, and life insurance payouts. Understanding the eligibility criteria, application process, and potential impacts on your finances is essential.

Social Security Benefits – If you are eligible for survivor benefits, contact the SSA to apply for them.

Employer Benefits – If applicable, inform your spouse's former employer to update or cancel any health insurance, pension, or other benefits.

4. Insurance Considerations

These can be significant, especially if your partner had life insurance policies or health insurance coverage that included you. Review your insurance policies, notify the relevant providers of your partner's passing, and assess how this affects your coverage and future insurance needs.

Health Insurance – Notify your health insurance provider of the change in your marital status. You may need to switch to an individual policy, possibly have Cobra coverage, or explore other options.

Auto and Home Insurance – Review and update your auto and home insurance policies, considering changes in coverage needs.

5. Housing and Living Arrangements

You may need to re-evaluate your living arrangements. You might consider downsizing, relocating, or modifying your current home to suit your needs as a single individual better. Housing decisions often tie into financial considerations, so careful planning is essential.

Home Ownership – Assess whether you wish to continue living in your current home or if downsizing or relocating is a more practical option.

Home Maintenance – Address any necessary home repairs or maintenance tasks that may have been deferred during the period of caregiving or illness.

6. Support Networks

Building and maintaining support networks are vital for emotional and practical assistance. Contact friends, family, and support groups to help you through the grieving process and offer assistance with daily tasks or emotional support.

7. *Self-care and Wellbeing*

Addressing practical life adjustments is vital, but don't overlook your own well-being. Self-care and well-being become paramount during this challenging time. Prioritize your physical and mental health by seeking professional help, maintaining a healthy lifestyle, and engaging in activities that bring you joy and relaxation.

Physical Health – Regular exercise and a balanced diet will help you maintain your physical health during this stressful time.

Mental Health – Grief counseling or therapy can provide valuable emotional support as you adapt to life without your spouse.

Self-Compassion – Practice self-compassion and allow yourself to grieve and heal at your own pace.

8. *Future Planning*

Planning for your future as you adjust to your new life is essential.

Goal Setting – Reflect on your personal goals and aspirations. Consider how you want to shape your life moving forward.

Rebuilding Connections – Reconnect with friends and interests that may have taken a back seat during your caregiving responsibilities.

Exploring New Possibilities – Be open to new experiences and opportunities that may arise as you continue your journey.

Finally, future planning is a forward-looking aspect that includes setting new goals, revising long-term plans, and considering your retirement and estate planning needs. Working with financial advisors and legal professionals can help you chart a secure and fulfilling future as you adapt to your life after losing your partner.

ELEANOR'S STORY

Eleanor had always been an active partner in her marriage. She and her husband, Henry, had shared the joys and responsibilities of their home for decades. But after Henry's passing, Eleanor faced a new reality: handling tasks that had once been their shared responsibility.

One sunny morning, Eleanor decided it was time to tackle one of these tasks – mowing the lawn. It was a chore she had never taken on, as it had always been Henry's domain. She stood before the lawnmower, feeling a mixture of trepidation and determination. The lawnmower seemed more significant and formidable without Henry's steady hand guiding it.

Eleanor started the lawnmower with a deep breath and began pushing it across the grass. At first, the machine felt unwieldy, and she had to wrestle with it to keep it on course. Memories of Henry's effortless maneuvers around the yard filled her mind, and tears welled up in her eyes.

But as Eleanor continued, something shifted inside of her. She thought about how Henry had always encouraged her to step out of her comfort zone, to try new things, and to be self-reliant. She realized that handling the lawnmower was not just a task. It was a symbol of her newfound independence.

With each pass, Eleanor grew more confident. The hum of the lawnmower became a comforting soundtrack, and the rhythm of her movements became fluid. She felt a connection to the earth beneath her feet, a connection that Henry had cherished during his time in the garden.

As she finished mowing the lawn, Eleanor wiped the sweat from her brow and looked at the neatly trimmed grass. She felt a profound sense of accomplishment and a bittersweet pride in her ability to handle this previously shared responsibility. It was a small step in her journey of self-reliance, but it was a significant one.

Eleanor knew that there might be more challenges ahead, more tasks to take on, and more moments when she would miss Henry's presence. But on that day, in the warm embrace of the sun and the roar of the lawnmower, she had taken the first step toward embracing her new role as a self-reliant widow, carrying her with the memory of a husband who had always believed in her strength and resilience.

EMBRACING NEW ROLES WITH RESILIENCE AFTER LOSING YOUR SPOUSE

Your world has been reshaped in so many profound ways. You are grieving and facing the task of taking on new roles and responsibilities that were once shared. While it's challenging, embracing your new roles with resilience can be a transformative journey toward personal growth and healing.

1. Acknowledge the Change

The first step in embracing new roles is acknowledging the change in your life. It's essential to recognize that the dynamics have shifted, and you are now responsible for tasks your spouse previously handled. This acknowledgment can be a sobering realization, but it's also the foundation upon which resilience I built.

2. Identifying Your Strengths

Every individual possesses a unique set of strengths and skills. Take the time to identify your own. You may discover talents and capabilities that you hadn't fully explored before. Recognizing your strengths will bolster your confidence as you take on new responsibilities.

3. Seeking Support

Embracing new roles doesn't mean you have to go it alone. Seek support from friends, family, or support groups who can offer guidance, practical assistance, and emotional comfort. Share your concerns and fears and allow others to lend a helping hand when needed.

4. Learning and Adapting

Resilience is born from adaptability. Approach new roles with a willingness to learn and adapt. You may need to acquire new skills or knowledge, whether managing finances, maintaining a home, or making decisions about your future. Don't be afraid to seek resources, such as classes or experts, to help you navigate these areas.

5. *Setting Realistic Expectations*

It's essential to set realistic expectations for yourself. Recognize that you may not excel in every new role immediately, and that's perfectly normal. Give yourself permission to make mistakes and learn from them. Resilience isn't about perfection but resilience in the face of challenges.

6. *Celebrating Small Wins*

As you take on new roles, celebrate even the most minor victories. Whether successfully managing a household task, making an important decision, or navigating a financial challenge, each accomplishment is a step forward. Acknowledge and reward yourself for your efforts.

7. *Fostering Self-Compassion*

Be kind to yourself throughout this process. Self-compassion means treating yourself with the same understanding and patience you would offer to a friend facing similar challenges. Understand that grief and adaptation take time, and it's okay to experience a range of emotions along the way.

8. *Finding Meaning and Purpose*

As you embrace new roles, consider how they fit into the broader context of your life. Finding meaning and purpose in these responsibilities can provide motivation and a sense of fulfillment. It can be an opportunity to honor your spouse's memory by living a life that aligns with your values.

9. *Reflecting on Resilience*

Take moments to reflect on your resilience. Consider the challenges you have already overcome and the strength you've discovered within yourself. Recognize that resilience isn't a fixed trait but a quality that can continue to develop and grow.

10. *Honoring Your Spouse's Legacy*

Embracing new roles can also be a way to honor your spouse's legacy. If your spouse encouraged your personal growth or had dreams for your future, consider how to carry those aspirations forward.

Embracing new roles with resilience after losing your spouse is undoubtedly a formidable challenge. It requires acknowledging change, identifying strengths, seeking support, and fostering self-compassion. Yet, it is also a journey of self-discovery, growth, and transformation.

As you navigate this path, remember that resilience is not a destination but a process. It's about learning, adapting, and finding the inner strength to face life's unexpected twists and turns. While the loss of your spouse is a harrowing experience, it can also be an opportunity to embrace new roles and discover the depth of your own resilience. In doing so, you honor your spouse's memory and create a future that reflects your own strength and capacity for growth.

THE THERAPEUTIC NATURE OF CREATING NEW ROUTINES

Creating new routines can be a therapeutic and transformative process in the wake of significant life changes. They provide structure, stability, and a sense of purpose during times of uncertainty and grief. We will now explore the benefits of establishing new routines and how they can contribute to healing and personal growth.

Losing a spouse is a life-altering event that leaves individuals feeling adrift in a sea of emotional turmoil. It disrupts the familiar rhythms of daily life and leaves a void where once there was companionship, shared responsibilities, and routines. In the face of such an upheaval, creating new routines offers stability.

Routines provide a predictable framework within which individuals can anchor themselves. They offer a semblance of control when other aspects of life may feel uncontrollable. Knowing what to expect at specific times of the day can bring a sense of order and comfort during turbulent times.

Grief can often lead to feelings of aimlessness and loss of purpose. The activities and responsibilities centered around the spouse may no longer exist. Creating new routines can help individuals regain a sense of accomplishment as tasks are completed. Over time, this can contribute to a renewed sense of accomplishment as tasks are completed. Over time, this can contribute to a renewed sense of purpose and meaning in life.

Grief is a rollercoaster of emotions, ranging from profound sadness to anger and confusion. New routines can serve as emotional anchors, helping individuals regulate their feelings and navigate the intensity of their emotions.

Engaging in familiar activities at specific times can provide stability during emotional fluctuation. For example, a morning walk, or meditation session can offer moments of calm and introspection, while an evening hobby or reading routine can provide a pleasant distraction from grief.

Creating new routines can also serve as a bridge between the past and the future. It allows individuals to hone the memory of their spouse while simultaneously looking forward to new experiences and opportunities.

Incorporating elements from the past, such as favorite activities or shared traditions, into new routines can be a way to cherish the memories of the spouse. At the same time, these routines can be vehicles for personal growth and exploration, helping individuals envision a future distinct from their past.

New routines can be designed to prioritize self-care and well-being. They provide dedicated time for activities that promote physical, emotional, and mental health. Whether it's daily exercise, meditation, journaling, or simply enjoying a favorite hobby, these routines contribute to overall well-being.

Prioritizing self-care through routines sends a powerful message of self-compassion. It emphasizes the importance of nurturing one's physical and emotional health during a challenging period of life.

Loss can often make individuals feel as though they have lost control over their lives. Creating new routines is an act of reclaiming control. It allows individuals to make deliberate choices about how they structure their days and activities.

Even in the face of profound loss, individuals can exert control over their routines. They can choose the pace at which they introduce new activities or adjust existing ones. This sense of control can be empowering and provide a sense of agency during a time of vulnerability.

So, it is not a static process but a dynamic one. It requires adaptability and the willingness to experiment with different activities and schedules. As individuals embark on this journey, they may discover new interests, strengths, and aspects of themselves they had not previously explored.

Over time, these evolving routines contribute to personal growth and resilience. They encourage individuals to step outside their comfort zone, take on new challenges, and expand their horizons.

So, in conclusion, the therapeutic nature of creating new routines in the aftermath of significant life changes, such as the loss of a spouse, cannot be overstated. These routines provide stability, purpose, emotional regulation, and connection to the past and future. They prioritize self-care, empower individuals, and foster adaptability and growth.

This is taking deliberate steps toward healing and personal growth. Your routines will offer a path to stability, purpose, and rediscovery of meaning in life.

8

REDISCOVERY: EMBRACING CHANGE AND GROWTH

"When I lost you, I felt unmoored and adrift. Now I know the winds and currents will bring me home again. You were not my anchor, but the water on which I float."

Change is one constant we can always count on in life's journey. Just as the seasons shift and the tides ebb and flow, our lives transform continuously. In these moments of change, we have the opportunity to rediscover ourselves, rekindle our passions, and embrace growth.

The journey of self-discovery post-loss is a deeply personal and often tumultuous path that individuals embark upon after experiencing the profound impact of loss. Whether it's the loss of a loved one, a relationship, a job, or any significant aspect of one's life, grief can be a powerful force that propels us into unchartered territory. In the wake of loss, we are forced to confront our vulnerabilities, fears, and the fragility of life itself.

At the outset, grief can be overwhelming and all-consuming. It can shroud us in darkness, making it challenging to envision a future without the pain of the past. However, as time progresses and you begin the healing process, the journey of self-discovery unfolds. It often starts with introspection and self-reflection as we grapple with questions about our identity, purpose, and the meaning of life. We may find ourselves reassessing our values, priorities, and the relationships that matter the most.

In this process, some individuals discover hidden reservoirs of resilience and strength they never knew existed. They learn to navigate the complex terrain of their emotions and develop a deeper understanding of themselves. The journey of self-discovery post-loss is not linear; it involves moments of both progress and setbacks. It requires patience, self-compassion, and the willingness to confront uncomfortable truths. It can be a process of shedding old layers of identity and beliefs that no longer serve us, paving the way for personal growth and trans-formation.

For many, this journey also leads to a greater appreciation for life's fleeting moments and a commitment to living more fully. It may inspire them to pursue long-neglected passions, seek new experiences, or channel their pain into creative outlets. Ultimately, the journey of self-discovery post-loss is a testament to the resilience of the human spirit, a profound exploration of the self, and a pathway toward healing and personal growth. Its challenges and revelations allow individuals to emerge from the shadows of grief into the light of a renewed sense of self and purpose.

Change can be both thrilling and terrifying. It can manifest in various ways, from the small, subtle shifts in our daily routines to the profound transformation that alters the course of our lives. Whether we welcome it with open arms or resist it with clenched fists, change is integral to our existence.

The paradox of change lies in its duality. It can bring uncertainty and discomfort but also promises renewal and growth. The choice to embrace or shy away from change often determines our ability to thrive in an ever-evolving world.

Rediscovery is reacquainting ourselves with who we are and what we value. It is a journey inward, a quest to uncover our true selves. Often, it begins with a moment of self-reflection, a pause in the frenetic pace of life when we ask ourselves, "Who am I now, and who do I want to become?

Embracing change requires us to be adaptable and open to new experiences. It calls for a willingness to let go of the old, even when it feels comfortable, and to welcome the unknown with curiosity and courage. Rediscovery is a voyage into uncharted territory where we shed the layers of our past selves and step into the potential of our future selves.

Life offers us a myriad of catalysts for rediscovery. Some are chosen, while others are thrust upon us. They may include career changes, relationship changes, or simply the passage of time. These catalysts serve as wake-up calls, urging us to reassess our priorities and values.

For Sarah, a successful corporate executive, it was a sudden health scare that prompted her to reevaluate her life. She realized that her relentless pursuit of professional success had left little room for personal well-being and meaningful relationships. This wake-up call led her on a journey of rediscovery, where she found solace in nature, cultivated deeper connections with loved ones, and pursued her long-lost passion for painting.

Nurturing neglected or new passions is a profoundly rewarding endeavor that can breathe life into our existence and provide a sense of purpose and fulfillment. Whether you've rediscovered a long-forgotten passion or stumbled upon an entirely new interest, the process of nurturing it involves a blend of dedication, curiosity, and self-discovery.

As we have mentioned, one of the first steps is to give yourself permission to explore and invest time in your passion. Life's demands often push our interests to the sidelines, but dedicating even a small portion of your day or week to your chosen pursuit can have a transformative impact. Be patient with yourself; passions need time to flourish, and progress may come in fits and starts.

Engaging in your passion can be a form of self-care and stress relief. It provides a sanctuary where you can escape the pressures of daily life and immerse yourself in something that brings you joy. Whether it's painting, writing, playing a musical instrument, gardening, or any other activity, the act of creation as a self-expression can be therapeutic and cathartic.

Moreover, nurturing neglected or new passions often leads to personal growth and self-discovery. As you delve deeper into your interests, you may uncover hidden talents, develop new skills, and gain a deeper understanding of yourself. Passion can be a mirror that reflects your values, desires, and dreams, and it can guide you toward a more authentic and fulfilling life.

Ultimately, nurturing passions is a lifelong journey that can infuse your life with vitality and purpose. It's a testament to your commitment to self-discovery and personal growth. Whether your passion becomes a lifelong pursuit or a source of joy in your daily routine, it can enrich your life in ways you may never have imagined. So, take this time to nurture those passions, both old and new, and let them become a vibrant thread in the tapestry of your existence.

Growth is the natural outcome of embracing change and embarking on the path of rediscovery. Just as a seed must break through its shell to sprout into a sapling, we, too, must break through the confines of our comfort zones to flourish. Growth requires a commitment to continual learning and self-improvement.

Courage lies at the heart of allowing oneself to evolve. It is the inner strength to confront the unknown, to venture beyond the confines of comfort zones, and to embrace change with open arms. Evolution is a constant process of growth and transformation that requires us to shed the old skin and step into the unfamiliar. This courageous act of self-discovery is an essential part of the human experience.

First and foremost, allowing oneself to evolve demands the courage to face one's fears and insecurities. Change often triggers a sense of vulnerability as we leave behind the familiar and tread uncharted territory. It takes courage to acknowledge these fears and take the first step toward personal growth. It's a leap of faith into uncertainty, where resilience and adaptability become our guiding lights.

Moreover, evolving requires the courage to challenge the status quo, including societal expectations, norms, and the opinions of others. It's about breaking free from the constraints of external influences and following the inner compass of authenticity. This process can be met with resistance from those who prefer the comfort of conformity, making the journey even more courageous.

Ultimately, allowing oneself to evolve is an act of self-compassion. It involves recognizing that you deserve growth, happiness, and a fulfilling life. It's about nurturing the belief that you are worth the effort and discomfort that change may bring. Each step forward is a testament to your inner strength.

In the end, embracing change and allowing oneself to evolve is a courageous choice to live a more authentic, fulfilling life aligned with one's true self. It is a declaration that your past does not define you; instead, you are shaping your destiny with the courage to grow and adapt to whatever challenges or opportunities come your way.

HERE IS A CASE STUDY: TRANSFORMATION POST-LOSS

Subject: Emily

Background:

Emily, a 38-year-old marketing executive, had always been deeply passionate about environmental conservation and sustainability. She had pursued a successful career in marketing, working for a prominent firm for over a decade. However, her life took an unexpected turn when she experienced the sudden loss of her father, who had been an avid environmentalist and her most significant source of inspiration.

The Catalyst for Change:

Emily's father's passing was a painful experience that prompted her to reflect deeply on her own life and values. She realized that her career in marketing, while financially rewarding, was not aligned with her true passions and the values she had inherited from her father. She felt a growing sense of discontent and needed a more meaningful and purpose-driven path.

The Transformation:

Emily's journey to rediscover herself and her true calling began with extensive research and self-reflection. She attended workshops and conferences on environmental conservation and volunteered with local organizations. This hands-on experience allowed her to connect with like-minded individuals who shared her passion. During this period, Emily also sought guidance from career counselors and mentors, who helped her explore various avenues within the field of environmental conservation.

Career Transition:

After several years of preparation, Emily made a drastic career change. She left her stable job in marketing and pursued a master's degree in environmental science and conservation. It was a challenging decision, requiring significant financial sacrifice and a willingness to start her career anew. However, Emily was determined to align her career with her values and honor her father's legacy.

Results:

Emily's transformation was not without its challenges. She faced a steep learning curve and financial instability during her academic pursuits. Nevertheless, her commitment to her newfound passion kept her motivated. After completing her degree, Emily secured a position with a respected environmental NGO where she could actively contribute to conservation efforts. Her work was rewarding and fulfilling, allowing her to make a meaningful impact on the causes she sincerely cared about.

9

LOVE AFTER LOSS: THE COMPLEX PATH TO NEW RELATIONSHIPS

"I know you don't want your death to be the defining moment of my life, and I'll try very hard to make sure it isn't."

A s the sun dipped in the horizon, casting a warm glow across the quiet park, Sarah sat alone on a weathered bench. It had been over a year since she lost her beloved husband, Mark, to a sudden illness. The pain was still there, a constant companion in her heart, but so was a growing realization that life must go on.

Sarah had hesitated for a long time before finally deciding to embark on this new journey. She had met James through a support group for those who had lost spouses, and over the months, they had become friends. Their conversations were a source of comfort, a lifeline to the world beyond her grief.

Tonight was different, though. James had asked her out on a date, and she had accepted, knowing it was time to take a tentative step forward. Her stomach churned with nervous anticipation. She had butterflies like a teenager about to experience her first crush.

As the appointed time drew near, Sarah was at the mirror, fumbling with her hair and makeup. She wore the beautiful aqua dress that Mark had once complimented, which she hadn't worn since his passing. The scent of her favorite perfume, a gift from him, lingered in the air.

With trembling hands, Sarah checked her reflection and whispered, "You can do this."

The restaurant they had chosen was cozy, with soft lighting and the comforting hum of conversations in the background. James was already waiting when she arrived, standing up as she approached.

"Sarah," he greeted her with a warm smile.

Sarah felt her heart skip a beat, a mixture of excitement and trepidation. She smiled back, feeling grateful for his kindness. They sat down, and for a while, the conversation flowed naturally. They shared stories, memories, and laughter as if they had known each other forever.

But then, like a looming storm cloud, the topic of their pasts emerged. James spoke about his late wife, Emily, with a hint of sadness in his eyes. Sarah listened intently, feeling the weight of her grief and the understanding they both carried.

As they continued to talk, Sarah felt a bond forming – a connection that transcended the pain of their shared losses. They spoke of their dreams, fears, and what they hoped to find in life.

James reached across the table when dessert arrived and gently took Sarah's hand. "I'm grateful for this evening, Sarah," he said softly. "I was scared to open my heart again, but being with you has been a wonderful surprise."

Sarah's eyes glistened with tears. "I feel the same way, James. It's been a long, painful journey, but maybe, just maybe, we can find a way to heal together."

They left the restaurant that night, hand in hand, their hearts still heavy with the memories of their last spouses but hopeful for the possibility of a new chapter in their lives. The stars above twinkled in approval as if to say that love and healing could bloom even after the darkest storms.

The experience of losing a spouse is one of the most emotionally devastating events a person can endure. It is a time marked by grief, longing, and profound sadness. Amidst this pain, it is not uncommon for individuals to deal with complex emotions, including feelings of betrayal. The myths of betrayal of a passed spouse often arise from a mix of grief, guilt, and the intricate web of human emotions.

MOVING ON MEANS FORGETTING:

One prevalent myth is that moving forward with one's life, which may involve finding love again or simply finding happiness, equates to forgetting or betraying the memory of the deceased spouse. This myth is rooted in the misconception that love is finite and that opening one's heart to new connections diminishes the love and respect held for the departed spouse. Finding joy again doesn't negate the love and cherished memories of the past. It simply acknowledges that life is a journey, and healing is part of it.

GUILT ABOUT NEW RELATIONSHIPS:

Surviving spouses often feel guilty when considering new romantic relationships. They may feel they are betraying their spouse by seeking companionship and love elsewhere. However, it's essential to understand that life continues, and human beings can love more than one person in their lifetime. Embracing new relationships doesn't diminish the love felt for the deceased spouse; instead, it's a testament to the resilience of the human heart.

HIDING FEELINGS:

Some individuals might believe they should suppress their feelings of attraction or affection towards someone new to remain loyal to their deceased spouse. They may think that acknowledging these emotions is a sign of disloyalty. However, it's important to remember that emotions are natural and should not be repressed. Accepting these feelings doesn't mean one is disloyal; it's a sign of emotional growth and the potential for new beginnings.

COMPARING NEW RELATIONSHIPS:

Another myth is that survivors should avoid comparing new relationships to their past ones. While it's essential not to dwell on caparisons, reflecting on the lessons learned from past relationships is entirely natural. These comparisons can help individuals make healthier choices in their new relationships, ensuring they grow and thrive.

HONORING THE PAST:

Some individuals might think honoring the past and embracing the future are mutually exclusive.

This myth suggests that remembering the deceased spouse should preclude forming new connections or finding joy. However, honoring the past and moving forward are not contradictory. Memories of the past can be cherished while making room for new experiences and connections in the present.

In reality, the human heart is vast and capable of simultaneously holding love, grief, and joy. In the context of a passed spouse, betrayal is often a misguided interpretation of complex emotions. It's essential to recognize that seeking happiness, forming new connections, or moving forward in life doesn't diminish the love and respect one holds for the spouse who has passed away. Instead, it reflects the remarkable resilience of the human spirit and the capacity to heal and find joy even after enduring enormous loss.

Dating after the loss of a spouse presents a set of unique challenges that can be emotionally and mentally taxing for the individual who is navigating this rugged terrain. Complex emotions and hurdles mark the journey from grief to finding love or companionship again. Here are some of the unique challenges of dating after a spousal loss.

Grief and Guilt:

Grief is a powerful and lasting emotion, and dating after the loss of a spouse can often lead to feelings of guilt. Survivors might feel as though they are betraying the memory of their deceased spouse by opening themselves up to new relationships. It's crucial to understand that finding love or companionship again is not betrayal but a natural part of the healing process.

Emotional Baggage:

Many individuals who have lost a spouse carry emotional baggage from their previous relationship. This could include unresolved grief, fear of loss, or lingering insecurities. These emotional scars can impact new relationships, making addressing and healing from them essential before fully opening up to someone new.

Comparison and Idealization:

It's natural to compare new potential partners to the deceased spouse. Sometimes, survivors may idealize their late spouse, making it challenging for new partners to measure up. This can create unrealistic expectations and hinder the development of new connections. This often happens without you realizing that you are doing it, so take the time to listen to what you are saying and choose your words carefully.

Social Pressure:

Friends and family members may unintentionally pressure widows and widowers to date again. While this can come from a place of concern and love, it can add additional stress to an already challenging process. People must be given the space and time to grieve and heal at their own pace.

Identity Shift:

Being part of a couple is a significant aspect of many people's identities. After losing a spouse, individuals may grapple with questions of identity and self-worth, particularly when considering dating again. Rebuilding one's identity as a single person or as part of a new couple can be complex.

Children and Family Dynamics:

For those with children, navigating dating after losing a spouse involves considering the impact on the family unit. Introducing a new partner into the lives of children can be challenging and requires thoughtful communication and sensitivity to everyone's needs.

Fear of Loss:

The fear of losing a new partner can be heightened for someone who has experienced the death of a spouse. The fear of going through that pain again can create emotional barriers in new relationships and hinder emotional intimacy.

Dealing With Triggers:

Certain places, objects, or anniversaries may serve as a trigger for memories of the deceased spouse. Navigating these triggers while building a new relationship can be emotionally challenging.

Disclosure and Communication:

Deciding when and how to disclose one's history of spousal loss can be challenging. Finding the right time and manner to share this aspect of one's life with a new partner requires careful consideration and communication.

Building Trust Again:

Trusting someone new after experiencing the profound loss of a spouse can be difficult. Learning to trust and be vulnerable with a new partner is crucial in building a healthy, loving relationship.

Despite these unique challenges, dating after the loss of a spouse is not only possible but can also be a path to healing and finding love and companionship once more. Individuals in this situation need to be patient with themselves, seek support when needed, and recognize that they deserve happiness and the opportunity to build new, fulfilling relationships while honoring the memory of their late spouse.

JOHN'S STORY

John had been a widower for five years since the passing of his beloved wife, Sarah. It had been a time of deep mourning, healing, and adjustment for both him and their two children, Emily and Michael. Life had moved on, albeit slowly, and John had recently met someone special, Lisa, who had captured his heart in a way he had not imagined possible.

The day had come for John to introduce Lisa to Emily, who was 16, and Michael, who was 12. He knew this moment was significant, a step towards blending their lives and forming a new family. John had thoughtfully planned the introduction, ensuring it would be in a comfortable and familiar setting for the children.

One sunny Saturday afternoon, John invited Lisa to join them for a picnic at their favorite park, a place filled with cherished memories of family outings with Sarah. As they set up the picnic blanket and unpacked sandwiches and snacks, John's heart raced with anticipation. He watched Emily and Michael play on the nearby swings, their laughter filling the air.

"Hey, you two," John called, his voice filled with warmth. "Come meet someone special to me."

Emily and Michael exchanged curious glances but obediently made their way over. John had prepared for this moment by explaining to them about Lisa, her kind nature, and the fact that she was a friend he had grown close to over time.

"Emily, Michael, this is Lisa," John said, introducing her with a warm smile. "Lisa, these are my children, Emily and Michael."

Lisa leaned down to their eye level, extending a friendly hand to each of them, "It's so nice to meet you both finally. Your dad has told me so much about you."

Emily nodded politely and said, "Hi," while Michael shyly mumbled a greeting.

The picnic continued, and as they ate, Lisa engaged in light conversation, asking Emily and Michael about their interests, school, and hobbies. She listened attentively, showing genuine interest in getting to know them.

As the afternoon unfolded, Emily and Michael gradually warmed up to Lisa. Emily began sharing stories about her school and her plans for the future while Michael asked questions about her favorite movies and hobbies. John watched with joy and relief, seeing the connection between his children and Lisa slowly forming.

After finishing their meal, they decided to explore the park further. Lisa suggested flying kites, a favorite pastime of hers. John and Lisa helped Emily and Michael assemble their kites, and soon, colorful shapes soared into the clear blue sky. Laughter filled the air again as they ran around, chasing the kites and each other.

As the sun began to dip below the horizon, John looked at Lisa, his heart swelling with gratitude. She had entered their lives patiently and kindly, trying to connect with his children without pushing too hard. He knew the journey to forming a blended family would have its challenges, but this day had been a promising start.

On the drive home, as Emily and Michael chatted about the fund they had, John held Lisa's hand and gave it a reassuring squeeze. He knew that introducing a new partner into their lives was a significant step, but today showed him that, with time and care, they could navigate this path together.

As they returned home, John felt a sense of hope for the future. Life had presented him with a second chance at love and happiness, and he was determined to make it work, not just for himself but for his children as well. Today was the beginning of a new chapter filled with possibilities and the promise of a loving, blended family.

As you can see, balancing past love with present possibilities is a delicate dance that many individuals engage in, especially when they have experienced the loss of a previous partner or the end of a significant relationship. It involves navigating the complex terrain of honoring cherished memories while remaining open to new connections and opportunities.

Embracing the Past: Past love holds a special place in our hearts. It's the repository of cherished memories, shared experiences, and the growth we've experienced through those relationships. We must embrace and honor this love, recognizing that it has shaped who we are today.

Learning from the Past: Past love offers valuable lessons. Whether a loving partnership or one filled with challenges, every relationship teaches us something about ourselves and what we desire in future connections. These lessons can guide us toward healthier, more fulfilling relationships in the present.

Healing from Loss: If the past love involved loss through death or separation, it's essential to allow oneself to grieve and heal. The healing process takes time, and it's important not to rush it. Healing doesn't mean forgetting; it means finding a way to move forward with love and memories intact and still a part of your life.

Opening Up to Possibilities: Present possibilities often come when we least expect them. Being open to new relationships or opportunities doesn't diminish the love we've experienced in the past. Instead, it acknowledges that life is a journey with room for multiple chapters and connections.

Balancing Memories and New Experiences: Balancing past love with present possibilities requires acknowledging that our hearts are expansive enough to love again. It's possible to create new memories and experiences without invading or erasing the love we've felt before. Each love story is unique and adds to the tapestry of our lives.

Communication is Key: Open and honest communication is vital if you're in a new relationship. Sharing your past and your feelings about it can help your partner understand your journey and provide support. It's also an opportunity to learn about their own experiences and perspectives.

Self-Care and Self-Reflection: Balancing past love with present possibilities involves self-care and self-reflection. Take the time to understand your own needs, desires, and boundaries. Knowing what you want from a new relationship can help you navigate it more effectively.

Support and Patience: Remember that this balancing act can sometimes be challenging. Seek help from friends, family, or even a therapist if needed. Be patient with yourself and your emotions, recognizing that feeling a mix of love, longing, and hope is okay.

Balancing past love with present possibilities is a profoundly personal journey; there is no one-size-fits-all approach. It's about finding what works for you, embracing the complexity of human emotions, and allowing your heart to guide you toward a future informed by the past and open to beautiful possibilities.

Dating is a deeply personal decision. Many times, it is accompanied by internal and external judgments. Navigating these judgments while pursuing the possibility of love and companionship can be challenging, but it is an essential part of the healing and growth process.

Your loved ones will have opinions about when and how a widowed person should start dating again. They may offer unsolicited advice or even criticism. While the intentions are good, remember that the decision is yours and a very personal one.

Society can impose expectations on how long after your loss you should or should not be dating. Again, these are often unrealistic and vary significantly from person to person. Listen to your heart. You are the only one who knows precisely what you are feeling.

Be kind to yourself. Understand that your journey has no "right" or "wrong" timeline for moving forward. If any of your feelings become overwhelming, seek professional help.

Don't be afraid to set boundaries when dealing with well-meaning family or friends. Let them know you appreciate their concern; your decisions in your personal life are just that, your decisions. Educate them about the grieving process, and advocate for your needs and desires regarding dating and seeking companionship.

Surround yourself with individuals who offer support, understanding, and encouragement. Engage with friends who have experienced similar losses, and you will find that these bonds are often incredibly beneficial.

Throughout this chapter, "Love After Loss: The Complex Path to a New Relationship," we have explored individuals' intricate and emotional journeys when considering the possibility of love and companionship. One thing becomes abundantly clear: finding love again is far from straightforward.

We have delved into the internal and external judgments accompanying this journey, including feelings of guilt, comparison, fear, and societal and familial expectations that can weigh heavily on those who have experienced loss. We've also examined the importance of self-compassion, Self-reflection, and setting boundaries in addressing these judgments.

Furthermore, we've explored the delicate balance between honoring the past and embracing present possibilities. It's crucial to remember that seeking happiness in connection with the present does not diminish the love and cherished memories of the past. It can be a way to honor and celebrate the love once shared.

Throughout this chapter, we've seen no one-size-fits-all approach after loss. Each person's journey is unique, shaped by their experiences, emotions, and healing process. It's a deeply personal path that requires patience, self-care, and a willingness to be vulnerable.

As we conclude this chapter, we leave you with the understanding that the pursuit of love after loss is a testament to the resilience of the human spirit. It's a journey that involves looking back with gratitude for what was and looking forward with hope for what can be. It's a complex path that offers the promise of healing, growth, and the possibility of finding love and companionship once more.

In the next chapter, we will continue to explore the various facets of love, relationships, and the human experience, acknowledging that each chapter in our lives, no matter how challenging, contributes to the beautiful tapestry of our individual stories.

10

LOVE AFTER LOSS: THE COMPLEX PATH TO NEW RELATIONSHIP

"On that day you left us, I realized that I'd loved you so well, I had not a single regret."

The air was filled with melancholy and hope in a quiet corner of a sun-dappled garden. Sarah, a woman with silver-streaked hair and a heart heavy with memories, stood alone beside a small, weathered oak tree. Today marked the fifth anniversary of her husband's passing, and she had chosen to honor his memory in a profoundly personal and touching ritual.

Their hands planted the oak tree on the day they moved into their first home together. It had witnessed their joys and sorrows, dreams and challenges, and it stood as a silent sentinel to their enduring love. In the years since her husband's death, the tree had grown and flourished, just as her memories of him had continued to bloom in her heart.

Sarah held a small, beautifully crafted wooden box in her hands. Inside, she had placed mementos of their life together. A faded photograph from their wedding day, a seashell they collected on their honeymoon, and a handwritten letter he had left for her before he passed. These treasures connected her to him, even in his absence.

With a trembling hand, she opened the box and began to speak. She spoke of their first meeting, the laughter they had shared, and the tears they had wiped away together. She spoke of the children they had raised and the dreams they had pursued side by side. Her voice cracked with emotion as she shared her longing for his presence and the emptiness she felt without him.

As she spoke, Sarah gently scattered rose petals around the base of the oak tree, each a symbol of the love that had blossomed and endured. She felt the sun's warmth on her face and the cool breeze rustling the tree's leaves. It was as if nature witnessed her tribute, offering solace and support.

When she finished, Sarah closed the box and placed it at the tree's base, nestled amongst the petals. She knew that her husband's spirit lived on in the tree's sturdy branches, in the rustling leaves, and in the memories they had created together. In this touching ritual, she found comfort and a sense of connection, knowing that even in his absence, their love would continue to bloom and flourish like the tree they had planted together.

As time goes by, you will establish ways of coming up with rituals and practices of remembering.

The days following the loss of a spouse are often filled with overwhelming grief and a profound sense of emptiness. During this heartache, establishing rituals and remembrances can provide solace and a way to honor the memory of your beloved partner. These rituals not only help you navigate the journey of grief but also allow you to celebrate the love and life you shared.

Here are some ways to help you with ideas about what to do.

CREATING A SPACE FOR REFLECTION

One of the first steps in establishing rituals is creating a dedicated space for remembrance. It could be a corner of your home adorned with photographs, mementos, and items with special meaning to you and your spouse. This space serves as a sanctuary where you can reflect, meditate, or feel close to your loved one. Lighting a candle or placing fresh flowers can add a soothing touch to this sacred space.

MARKING SIGNIFICANT DATES

Anniversaries, birthdays, and other significant dates can be incredibly challenging after the loss of a spouse. Consider establishing rituals for these occasions that allow you to celebrate your partner's life. Lighting a candle, visiting a favorite place, or sharing stories with loved ones can help you commemorate these special moments and keep your spouse's memory alive.

KEEPING A MEMORY JOURNAL

A memory journal is a powerful way to capture and preserve your thoughts, emotions, and memories of your spouse. Dedicate a notebook or use a digital platform to record your reflections, anecdotes, and feelings. Writing can be a therapeutic outlet for your grief, and reading through your journal over time can help you track your healing journey and witness your resilience.

ESTABLISHING ACTS OF KINDNESS

Honoring your spouse's memory can extend beyond personal rituals. Consider establishing acts of kindness in their name.

Whether donating to a cause they were passionate about, volunteering in their memory, or simply performing small acts of kindness, these actions can create a lasting legacy and bring a sense of purpose to your grief.

SHARING STORIES AND TRADITIONS

Sharing stories about your spouse with friends and family can be a beautiful way to keep their memory alive. Encourage loved ones to share their anecdotes and memories, creating a collective tapestry of remembrance. You can also consider adopting meaningful traditions with your spouse, such as cooking their favorite meal on special occasions or revisiting places you both cherished.

Establishing rituals and remembrances is a personal and evolving process. There is no right or wrong way to honor your spouse's memory, and it's essential to allow yourself the flexibility to adapt these rituals as you navigate the complexities of grief. Ultimately, these acts of remembrance can provide comfort and connection, allowing you to find moments of peace and healing amid loss.

Your family will appreciate the memories and will enjoy the stories. Or just speaking of him and knowing it's okay to do that around you. People often don't know what to say, so tell them it's okay if they talk about them to you. That keeps their memory alive.

Many times, during the depths of grief and loss, memories can be both a balm and a source of pain. They are fragile threads that connect us to the past, to the ones we've loved and lost. While memories can sometimes bring tears, they also possess a profound healing power, offering solace, comfort, and a means of keeping the spirit of our loved ones alive.

Memories serve as time capsules that preserve the essence of our loved ones long after they are gone. The sound of their laughter, the twinkle in their eyes, and the warmth of their embrace become treasures we can revisit whenever we need them. In the quiet corners of our minds, we can relive the love, joy, and shared experiences that define our relationships.

Think about a tattered, old blanket you must have in the winter. It not only offers warmth but having that blanket also offers comfort. Memories provide familiarity in a world that has been altered by loss. When we recall the routines, inside jokes, and shared traditions, we are reminded of the stability and constancy our loved ones brought into our lives. These memories provide a sense of continuity and help us navigate the turbulent waters of grief.

As we grapple with grief, the ability to remember becomes an act of resilience. The simple act of reminiscing can be a powerful way to cope with loss. It reminds us that, even in our pain, we carry our loved ones with us, and their influence continues to shape our lives.

Establishing rituals around memories can be a therapeutic way to harness their healing power. Lighting a candle on an anniversary, visiting a favorite spot, or writing letters to our loved ones are all acts that breathe life into our memories. These rituals provide a sense of connection and allow us to express our enduring love. Find what works for you. Find what offers you solace while keeping the memories alive.

Memory has the extraordinary ability totranscend time and space. It enables us to bridge the gap between the past and the present, making it feel like our loved ones are still with us. In this way, memory becomes a bridge that allows us to keep their presence alive in our hearts.

Sharing memories with others who knew and loved our departed can be a profound experience. It allows us to collectively celebrate and commemorate our loved ones, thus reinforcing the idea that they are not truly gone as long as they live on in our hearts and our stories.

So, remembering can be compared to an art form. In the darkest moments of grief, memory is a way to sculpt the past into something beautiful and enduring. It requires patience, tenderness, and self-compassion. As we cherish our memories, we transform them into a source of strength, a tribute to the love that once was, and a testament to our capacity to heal.

The healing power of memory doesn't just live in what we remember but how we remember. Through our eyes, we can find hope, inspiration, and the courage to move forward. Through the tapestry of memories, we discover the profound truth that love endures, even in the face of loss.

Many countries have different ways of remembering and celebrating the lives of their people. Here are just a few for you to read about.

JAPANESE HANAMI FOR ANCESTORS

In Japan, the annual tradition of Hanami, or cherry blossom viewing, is a celebration of the fleeting beauty of cherry blossoms and a way to honor ancestors. Families gather beneath the blossoming cherry trees to enjoy food and drinks, and they often bring along photographs or personal items of their deceased loved ones. They believe that the spirits of their ancestors visit during this time, and by sharing food and stories beneath the blossoms, they show respect and remember their family members who have passed away.

MEXICAN DIA DE LOS MUERTOS OFRENDAS

Dia de los Muertos, or the Day of the Dead, is a vibrant and colorful celebration in Mexico that takes place from October 31st to November 2nd. Families create ofrendas, or altars, dedicated to deceased loved ones. These altars are adorned with marigold flowers, sugar skulls, candles, and the favorite foods and beverages of the departed. Families also place photographs and mementos of the ofrendas to welcome the spirits of the deceased back into their homes. It's a joyous celebration of life and a way to remember and honor those who have passed.

BUDDHIST LANTERN FLOATING IN JAPAN

In Japan, a tradition called Toro Nagashi, or lantern floating, is often associated with Buddhist ceremonies. People write messages or prayers on paper lanterns and then float them on rivers, lakes, or the sea. This act symbolized the journey of the souls of the deceased to the afterlife. It's a serene and contemplative way to honor and remember loved ones while offering blessings and well wishes for their spiritual journey.

GHANAIAN FANTASY COFFINS

In Ghana, particularly among the Ga people, the tradition of fantasy coffins is a unique way to celebrate the lives of the deceased. These coffins are custom-made in the shape of objects or symbols representing the person's profession, interests, or passions. For example, a fisherman might be buried in a coffin shaped like a fish, while a teacher might have one resembling a book. This tradition is a colorful and creative way to honor and remember the deceased's individuality.

SOUTH KOREAN CHUSEOK ANCESTRAL RITUALS

During Chuseok, the Korean harvest festival, families come together to pay their respects to their ancestors through a Charye ritual. They prepare a table with various dishes and offerings and perform a series of bows and gestures to express gratitude to their ancestors for their blessings and guidance. This ritual underscores the importance of family and maintaining a connection with one's heritage. It's a way to honor those who came before and paved the way for future generations.

These examples showcase the rich diversity of cultural traditions for honoring the deceased, emphasizing the universal desire to remember and pay respect to those who have passed away. Each tradition carries its unique symbolism and significance, reflecting the values and beliefs of the respective cultures.

Life is a precious and finite gift, and one of the most profound ways to honor the memory of a loved one is by embracing this gift with gratitude and living it to the fullest. Here, we will explore how to seize the beauty of life, even in the face of loss, and make the most of every moment.

Gratitude as a Daily Practice

Begin each day with a grateful heart. Take a moment to reflect on the simple joys, the people you cherish, and the opportunities surrounding you. Gratitude opens your eyes to the abundance in your life and is a powerful reminder of the gift of living.

Pursue Your Passions

What are the dreams and passions that ignite your soul? Whether it's a long-held aspiration or a new interest, pursue it with dedication and enthusiasm. Your loved one's memory can be a guiding light, encouraging you to follow your heart and embrace your unique journey.

Cultivate Meaningful Relationships

Life is enriched through connections with others. Nurture your relationships with friends, family, and loved ones. Invest time and effort into building deep and meaningful connections that bring joy, love, and support into your life.

Take Risks and Embrace Change

Don't be afraid to step out of your comfort zone and take calculated risks. Change is a natural part of life's unfolding story, and by embracing it, you open yourself up to new experiences, growth, and transformation.

Practice Mindfulness

Live in the present moment with mindfulness and awareness. Let go of worries about the past or anxieties about the future. By immersing yourself in the here and now, you can deeply savor life's experiences.

Seek Adventure and Exploration

Life is an adventure waiting to be explored. Travel, try new activities, and expand your horizons. Discover the beauty of different cultures, landscapes, and perspectives. Every unique experience is a treasure.

Give Back to Others

One of the most fulfilling ways to embrace the gift of life is by giving back to others. Volunteer, support a cause, or perform acts of kindness. Helping others spreads positivity and brings a profound sense of purpose.

Celebrate Milestones and Achievements

Take pride in your accomplishments, both big and small. Celebrate your milestones with enthusiasm and acknowledge your hard work and dedication. Your loved one would want to see you reveling in your achievements.

Forgive and Let Go

Forgiveness is a powerful tool for freeing yourself from the burdens of the past. Holding onto grudges or resentment only hinders your ability to live life fully. Release the weight of negative emotions and allow yourself to move forward with a lighter heart.

Cherish the Beauty of Nature

Spend time in nature and marvel at its beauty. Whether it's a serene walk in the woods, watching a sunset, or feeling the sand between your toes at the beach, connecting with the natural world can rejuvenate your spirit.

Stay Curious and Keep Learning

A curious mind keeps life vibrant and exciting. Continue to learn, explore new interests, and seek knowledge. The pursuit of learning is a lifelong journey that can bring endless joy and fulfillment.

Reflect and Reconnect

Regularly reflect on your life's purpose and values. Reconnect with your inner self to ensure that your choices and actions align with what truly matters to you. This introspection can guide you toward a life filled with purpose and authenticity. By embracing the gift of life and living to the fullest, you honor the memory of your loved ones and find solace, joy, and meaning in the midst of grief. Life is a precious and fleeting journey; by making the most of it, you create a beautiful legacy of your own.

As our journey through these pages concludes, life's journey, with its memories and hopes, continues ever onward.

AFTERWORD

Emily's case study illustrates the transformative power of personal loss as a catalyst for career change. Through introspection, education, and unwavering determination, she was able to pivot from a successful career in marketing to a fulfilling role in environmental conservation. Her journey is an inspiring example of how individuals can find purpose and meaning by aligning their careers with their true passions, even in the face of profound personal loss. Emily's story reminds us that our most significant growth sometimes occurs when we bravely step onto a new path forged from the ashes of adversity.

In the grand tapestry of life, change is the thread that weaves through every chapter. Rediscovery is acknowledging that change and embracing it is an opportunity for growth. It is a lifelong journey that invites us to peel back the layers of our identity, uncover our true selves, and nurture our potential.

As you embark on your journey of rediscovery, remember that change is not to be feared but embraced. It is the chisel that sculpts the masterpiece of your life. Embrace change, rediscover yourself, and watch as you grow into the person you were always meant to be. In the words of the ancient philosopher Heraclitus, "Change is the only constant in life." Embrace it, and you will find your most genuine self along the way.

REFERENCES

Psychological Adjustment to Sudden and Anticipated Spousal Loss Among
Older Widowed Persons
Journals of Gerontology, Series B, Volume 56, Issue 4
1 July 2001 Pages S237-S248
Https:/doi.org/10.1093/geronb/56.4, S237
Lovetoknow.com
45 Plus Sudden Death Quotes of Peace and Comfort
Kate Miller-Welson Pub May 7, 2021

Printed in Great Britain
by Amazon

37835847R00086